God
LOVES
India

Celebrating 50 years of
powerful ministry in India

# God
## LOVES
# India

Celebrating 50 years of
powerful ministry in India

**Bill and Joyce Scott**
*with* **Bill Teate**
*as told to* **Donald Grey Barnhouse, Jr.**

**Whitaker House**

Unless otherwise indicated, all Scripture quotations are taken from the *King James Version* (KJV) of the Holy Bible.

Scripture quotations marked (NIV) are from the Holy Bible, *New International Version*, © 1973, 1978, 1984 by the International Bible Society. Used by permission.

Scripture quotations marked (NKJV) are from the *New King James Version,* © 1979, 1980, 1982 by Thomas Nelson, Inc. Used by permission. All rights reserved.

## GOD LOVES INDIA

For more information, or to be put on the
Scotts' mailing list, please contact:

India Bible Literature/Scripture Ministries of India
22 South Main Street
Dover, PA 17315
Phone: 717.292.0100 • Fax: 717.292.0335
E-mail: doragaru@aol.com

ISBN: 0-88368-636-8
Printed in the United States of America
© 1999 by Donald Grey Barnhouse, Jr.

Whitaker House
30 Hunt Valley Circle
New Kensington, PA 15068

1 2 3 4 5 6 7 8 9 10 11 12 / 09 08 07 06 05 04 03 02 01 00

# Contents

## Dedication

*Unto him who loved us
and washed us from our sins
in his own blood.*

—Revelation 1:5

# Chapter 1

# How I Got Involved

**D**onald Barnhouse: This book is the story of a work of God so large, and in such a difficult place, that I was in awe, tempted to disbelief, when I heard about it. Investigation led to conviction, and a strong desire to have more people hear about it. It is exciting and inspiring. It can give you courage for your own work, anywhere, large or small.

From the time when I began to realize the scope of the work that God has accomplished through Bill and Joyce Scott, however, I found myself seeing the story in two very different ways at the same time. In one way it was a story about India: elephants, tigers, and cobras, pitiful beggars and the Taj Mahal, cows treated as holy and children sold into prostitution, corruption and pride, the ancient caste system and modern nuclear weapons, close to a billion people in a vast and alien nation. But in another way this story was about two individuals you might pass in the street without noticing.

Many people live their lives on the basis of the question "What can I do?" They act, or fail to act, on the basis of "What do you expect me to do? What can one person do?" The story of Bill and Joyce Scott is the story of two people who lived by a different outlook. They stood on, *"Is anything too hard for the* Lord*?"* and, *"If God be for us, who can be against us?"* (Genesis 18:14; Romans 8:31). The result has been that these two have been used to bring about radical changes in the lives of literally millions, in a land where most people think change is next to impossible.

One of the numbers that stands out in my mind most vividly is two million. Two million was the number of children who were in Vacation Bible School in India in 1996 directly through their work. I know a pastor who was excited when he managed to get thirty children in a Pennsylvania neighborhood into his church's VBS one summer.

The Scotts have built up their Vacation Bible Schools in just a few years, and expect that number of two million to go still higher, perhaps before this book reaches you.

When Bill Teate arranged for me to meet and talk with Bill and Joyce Scott, I had a strange sense of double vision. There we were, four of us in a small room together, but in my mind's eye I saw two million children, two million little foreign faces from a country I would have given up on as hopelessly steeped in superstition and demon worship. Then, right in front of me I saw Bill and Joyce, sitting in two chairs in a motel room near Lancaster, Pennsylvania.

Should I try to describe them to you? I think not. Appearances can be very misleading. As I said, you might pass them in the street without a second glance. But after looking at either one of them for any length of time, you would become aware of seeing something far beyond their appearances. For me, the picture of Bill Scott first began to come clear through his eyes. I never saw a pair of eyes that manage to look so determined and so kind at the same time.

The true picture of Joyce started to form in my mind through noticing something about her posture. She always looked ready. I sensed that nothing could ever frighten or fluster her. Both have a look of no-nonsense capability. Both have a look of keen intelligence without any need to prove it. No one who gets to know them can miss sensing their godliness, integrity, and commitment.

In planning for our meeting, I looked forward to learning both stories: the story of the millions and the story of the two. I want you to meet them first on the field, doing what they love best. Then, we will "flash back" to see how God called them, how they got to India, and how he brought their lives together. Finally, we will return to India and see more of what God has been doing through their work.

In many of the conversations there was laughter mixed in with the answers. You will have to imagine the laughter, but here are the words, edited only slightly from the way they spoke them to me.

*— Donald Grey Barnhouse, Jr.*

# Chapter 2

# A Taste of India

**B**ill *Scott*: Let me tell you why we went to villages. Both Joyce and I had the same reason. I did not know Joyce when she was making the choice as to what mission to go to in India, and she did not know me, but I chose the India Mission for the same reason that Joyce did. We looked at all the missions and what their primary goals were, and the primary goal of the India Mission was to go to the 85% of the people who live in rural areas of India, not the cities. We chose a mission that had as its primary thrust the villages of India.

So the school where we were first assigned was totally rural. We started out in a small village.

*DB*: And where were you living?

*Bill*: We were living in a rented house, the same kind of a house that our teachers rented. At that time, we're talking in the fifties, that was a radical move, because at that time the general way was that missionaries lived in a compound, which had a wall and out of which they worked, and the nationals lived outside. We refused to go to the mission compound. There was a mission house in the area where we were sent, and we had the right to ask for it, but we didn't. We didn't want it. We chose to live in a rented house the same as that in which our teachers were living. So that was a choice.

*DB*: When we read the word "house," we have an image in mind of a roof, walls, a door, windows, and all of that. Tell us about this house.

*Bill*: Well, do you want to describe the house, Joyce?

*Joyce Scott*: It would be better if you did, because, ah, you didn't accept it very well. You'd better tell all your points.

DB: All right, Bill, I'm braced. What kind of house was it?

Bill: That's a good question. When you say house, maybe within the minds of western readers there may be a concept that is certainly not the concept of what a house is out in the village. I'm trying to remember the first house that we went to in Peddapalli, if I recall it correctly. Joyce has a better memory of these things.

Joyce: It was the little white one.

Bill: Oh, yes, between the station and the school.

Joyce: During the rainy season, every room, every ceiling in every room, leaked. Except the bathroom.

Bill: Yes, and even though I came from Ireland, the land of rains, and had lived in a very small house, it wasn't a house that leaked, and this one did. We literally had to have umbrellas inside the house. The only room that didn't leak was the bathroom, so I spent a lot of time there. Maybe that's where I got the habit of reading and doing my studying in that room.

But I must tell you that the bathroom, of course, was not a bathroom like those we know here. It was a room where we didn't have a flush toilet, right?

Joyce: That's right.

Bill: It didn't have a flush toilet, and it had to be cleaned out by people every day…

Joyce: By "sweepers."

Bill: The people the Indians call "sweepers" are the most despised and neglected. We didn't have electric lights, and we certainly didn't have air conditioning, or even any fans, although the temperature was in the 90 to 100 degree range.

DB: Was there a shower?

Bill: A shower? There was a big stone pot full of water. You dipped a can in it and poured the water over you. That was our shower—unheated. But we didn't want heated water, actually. When it was over 90 degrees, that water felt good. So that was our shower. One time Joyce discovered a snake when she was lifting up…

Joyce: Not there!

Bill: No, in another house, but that same kind of stone pot. Anyway, that's the kind of house. All stone floors…

Joyce: …what we called *shava*. Put together with cement, you know, a block here, and a block like that.

Bill: But it was a house like those in which our teachers lived. So now, these teachers have grown with us, and they know what we lived in.

DB: What kind of food did you eat there?

Bill: Mostly Indian food, and the vegetables that were available in the village, of course. We were in a village, so we didn't have a selection of vegetables. In a village in India, you eat the crop that is prevalent at that particular season. So one time you're eating all *brinjal*, the next time you're eating all onions,…

Joyce: *Brinjal* is eggplant.

Bill: Another time, all tomatoes.

Joyce: The kitchen was separate from the house, by the way. It was sort of an outhouse type of thing.

Bill: The food was cooked there, and we had to eat it in the house.

Joyce: After a while we began to look for another place. We went down towards the railroad, and we found a huge rice mill there. In the rice mill, there was a big building. Some Parsees and some Jains lived there. The Jains lived on the top floor, and there were a couple of rooms free—two rooms and a little outhouse for the kitchen—were free on the first floor.

Bill: There we had another snake story. Tell it, Honey.

Joyce: Well, we were in these two great big rooms. Each one was about three-fourths the size of a normal American motel room, and we had everything we owned in those two rooms. For the bathroom, we had to go outside to a place like an old fashioned outhouse. One day when I went in, there was a big cobra. It had taken up residence in the toilet. So we had to make a place inside for our bathing.

DB: What did you do about the cobra?

Joyce: We just let him be. Everybody was saying, "What

are you going to do? What are you going to do?" Eventually, we prayed him out.

Then just a couple of weeks after that, on a Saturday morning, Bill had gone over to the school when I heard our cook call out, "Snake! Snake! Snake!" I went out the back and asked, "What's up?" They answered, "There's a snake here." So I asked, "Where is it?" "It's in our house." It was in a servant's little house. I looked and asked, "Where?" "There, over there."

Now, the people there don't have closets and cupboards like we do. They don't have regular beds like we do or anything. They just sleep on the floor, and they have little boxes, like little tin suitcases, that they have their things on. They had this old dilapidated table, four legged, with boxes on top of it. They said, "The snake's behind there!" And the cook said, "Oh, big cobra!"

I took a look between the wall and the table, and I bent down and looked some more, but all I could see was the loop of the snake. I couldn't see where its head was. Everybody was screaming, including a bunch of kids who were there. So I tried to get everybody out. Then I brought in the fellow who carried water. By the way, the only running water that we had was the fellow with the pail, when he was running with it.

I called to him, "Come on, Mark," and I saw he was shaking. His knees were like spaghetti. I said, "Get me the crowbar." They got the crowbar, and I looked under that table, and I just took aim at that loop. The problem was that I didn't know where the head was, or how much body there was between the loop and the head. I was thinking, "If I'm going to hit him here, how much snake is going to come after me?"

Well, it had to be done, so I just aimed and hit him, pinning him against the wall with the crowbar. There was a lot of jerking and thrashing about as he dropped from behind there, and I was just looking to see what was going to come after me. It turned out I had hit him about three feet behind his head. So I gave the crowbar to Mark to hold. "Hold it, Mark, and don't let go!" I went for an axe, and I chopped at its body against the wall. It was just like rubber, but I finally punctured its back, and blood began to spurt. So I jumped back, and I said, "Okay, Mark, you drop the crowbar and jump back." The snake came out after us, but I knew that it could not jump much because of its broken back. So then I took the crowbar and laid it across the snake to pin it down, and I asked Mark to stand on this crowbar. Then I took the axe and killed it.

Bill Teate:[1] You axed it no questions!

Joyce: Right! And it was about eight feet long. We carried it out and put it on our back veranda. When our cat came out after awhile and saw it, she walked up to it gingerly, took one step back, arched her back with her hair standing straight up, and went screeching out of the place.

DB: Tell me about the Parsees and the Jains.

Joyce: They are among the minor religions. Less than 1% of the people in India are Parsee, and about the same number are Jains. Parsees are those who worship fire.

DB: Parsees—a corrupted remnant of the Persian Zoroastrians?

Joyce: Yes, exactly right. The Jains are those who worship all the animals. Instead of killing that snake, they would have fed it. I knew the people upstairs were Jains, but they didn't say anything to me.

DB: Where did you go after living in your temporary rooms in that warehouse?

Joyce: We found another little house, where we hoped we would not have to contend with all the leaks. We moved in on a Saturday morning when we didn't have classes. We had twin beds, and that night we had put our mosquito nets in place, and Bill had gone into the bathroom. Again, the floors were that *shava* stone. The walls were mud and brick, with plaster

---

[1] Bill Teate is a long-time friend of the Scotts and assists their ministry by facilitating partnerships between Christians in the United States and India Bible Literature.

over them, lime plaster.

There was no electricity and no running water. The bedroom opened into the dining room, and in back of that was the kitchen. Opposite the kitchen was the bathroom, and beyond that was the toilet, which was a little room with the toilets in it. They were just chairs, little stools with pots that were cleaned every day.

Well, Bill called me, so I went in, and he said, "Joyce, look down there, What kind of dirt is that?" I looked on the floor, and having been interested in biology when I was in high school, I said, "Hmm, that's snake dirt."

Now, in Ireland they had no snakes, so Bill wouldn't understand what that was. I just quietly looked up. Above me, where I could have reached up and touched it with my hand, was a snake in the rafters of that bathroom. The rafters are just sort of clay pieces put together like tiles, and then clay put over them. If you poke them with a stick, your stick will go right through the roof. So I couldn't jab at the snake. Also, with only kerosene light, we couldn't see how long it was. Plus, if I had attacked him when he was above me, he could have just dropped on me to attack me.

DB: Did you recognize what kind of snake it was?

Joyce: It was a male cobra. I said, "Well, Bill, I don't think we can do anything. You finish bathing, and I'll watch him." Then he watched, and I finished.

In those houses they have little drain holes under the frame of the door, so that you can just swish water back and forth. That's what they call washing the floors. They just pour water, swish it around, and then push it through. So we stuffed the drain holes as tightly with newspaper as we could. We closed all the doors and stuffed every place we could think of to keep that animal in there. We stuffed paper between the back door and the dining room, and between the dining room and the bedroom, and then we got under the nets, hopeful that would take care of it. The story has a dull ending: nothing happened. We slept, and the next morning when we looked, it wasn't there. That was our first night there in that house.

DB: That's not a dull ending; that's a happy ending!

Joyce: Actually it wasn't quite the end. We had what is called a "back-door dispensary." People come saying, "I've got a tummy-ache," or "I've got a headache," or "I've got diarrhea," and they want missionaries to do the "back-door dispensary." You give them medicine. About three weeks after that first night, somebody had been there at noon. We'd come home and had our lunch. Then the cook, Samuel, told me that there was somebody there. I took care of that person and came in to wash my hands. We had just a little basin of water, a little white agate basin, you know. I dipped up some water and put it in there. As I was washing my hands, I heard some gravel fall. I was scared, and I slowly looked up, sort of sideways, and there was that snake, that male cobra, going along the ledge of that bathroom, just under the edge of the rafters, maybe a foot or two away.

Bill: Very close.

Joyce: I called, "Bill! Bill!" But he was in the front of the house and didn't hear anything. I called, "There's a snake here! Come here!" He still didn't hear anything. I was screaming for help.

Samuel, our cook, is a dear old man. He's almost deaf, but he did hear my screaming, so he came. I yelled, "Get me the crowbar! Get me the crowbar!" When he came back with it and saw the snake he said, "Ooooohhh!" I said, "Shush, just a minute." So I took the crowbar, as I had before, and I pinned that snake against the wall there. Immediately it was thrashing, of course. This time I held the crowbar and told Samuel to get me the axe. So he ran outside, looked around, and brought the axe back in. We usually had an axe for chopping wood for the wood stove. I kept calling for Bill, but Bill didn't hear. Then I told Samuel to take hold of the crowbar and hold it, whatever he did. So I used the axe on it and killed it.

DB: And that finally was the end of that?

Joyce: Not quite. I was concerned because female cobras,

they say, will chase people who kill the male cobras.

DB: Rudyard Kipling said so.

Joyce: Well, that was in my mind. We had several adventures with cobras, male and female, while we were at that house. The day we were leaving to go to a different place, curled up in front of our door on our front doorstep just outside the screen door, was a huge female cobra. We couldn't get out. We could just look at her through the screen.

DB: By huge, what do you mean?

Joyce: Oh, at least ten feet. So I thought, "Okay, now what do we do?" In our end room we had about ten girls we had brought up from Bhongir. The mission had a girls' school there that was not recognized. Our school was getting recognized, and the mission wanted those girls to come into our school so that they could go on to other schools. If a school didn't have the official recognition from the government, the students couldn't go on to high school or college. So that's what we were working for.

Bill: There are stiff qualifications for recognition, which the schools didn't have until Joyce came there, and then she brought them up to that point of recognition.

Joyce: So here were these girls all saying, "*Pamu, pamu!*" "Snake, snake." So I went back into the house, got the tools, came out the back door and around the house. When I got to the front, the snake was gone. That was one I didn't have to take care of. But they are dangerous. An American was visiting us one time, and he found a cobra snake down a hole. He stuck a stick in there and was teasing it, and that snake came right on up and chased him.

Bill: Fast! He ran as fast as he could!

Joyce: He never ran so fast, and he got in the door barely two steps before the snake got there. I said, "Bob, we said…"

Bill: I had told him, "Don't do that!"

Joyce: Then we got a Siamese cat. A few times when we had gone out in the evening and come back, there were dead snakes on our front veranda—smaller snakes, but dead ones—

as we walked in. She was the only living being in the house, so she was killing them. She knew to kill poisonous snakes.

Bill: This village was right out on the edge of the jungle, you see. We were really out in rural India.

Joyce: Scorpions, snakes. Bill got stung there.

Bill: I was stung a couple of times by a scorpion.

DB: Why didn't it kill you?

Joyce: Because it wasn't the lethal kind.

Bill: They're painful, but not always lethal.

Joyce: There's the lethal kind. Like the kind that you caught, those are lethal.

DB: Did you step on one and get stung on your foot?

Bill: No, on my wrist. When I was opening our gate. It had a lock that you pull up, and as I was pulling it up, I felt the stinger going in. It felt just like a needle going in, and immediately I let go, of course, and it dropped. Then I came in and…

Joyce: Suffered pain for twenty-four hours.

Bill: Yes! As I announced, "A scorpion stung me just now," the pain went right through my body. It's a twenty-four hour period, and almost twenty-four hours to the minute later, it stopped.

DB: Weren't you afraid that it was a poisonous scorpion?

Bill: Not really. I mean, we had the power of prayer and trusted God. We couldn't tell what kind it was, because I didn't even see it. It got away. I didn't kill it. I was hurting, but not unduly alarmed at that point. I wasn't terrifically afraid. And then, interestingly, I don't know whether this is what always happens, but my second sting—that time I did see the scorpion, and it stung me on my finger—did not hurt nearly as much as the first. It was almost, oh, less than half as bad. Maybe I was inoculated by the first sting. I'm not sure.

# Chapter 3

# The Missionary Vision

**B**ill: My heart, my desire, was and is to get the Word of God to the whole nation of India. I went to India with a burden to go to the rural areas, because the research showed us that's where the people of India lived, 85% of them, and that's where the need was, and that's where the fewest missionaries were. Most of the missionaries were concentrated in the cities, with the smaller percentage of the people. So my burden was for the people of the villages, and then later, I found that was also Joyce's burden. So we had a mutual burden for rural India.

Joyce: We were married on January 8, 1952. We learned later that was the day that the young missionaries were killed in Ecuador by the Aucas. Then we did our second year of language study, and after that was finished we were assigned to go work in a boarding school, because I was a teacher and Bill was trained in business, accounting and all that. The students were the sons and daughters of evangelists who were working with India Mission.

Instead of living on a missionary compound, we rented an Indian house. That's where Bill was walking down the dusty roads into the small bazaar there, and that's where his story begins—with what he saw on the shelves in the bazaar.

Bill: Even before that, actually. While I was studying language, I shared with the senior missionary on the station my burden to get God's Word to the people of India. I didn't have at that point a clear vision from God, but I had a burden from God: to get Scriptures and Christian books to the rural people.

So I said to the missionary, "I don't see any Christian

books," to which he replied, "We have none in Telugu, and any English ones we have are what we've brought from America." When I asked, "Well, why don't we get Christian books into the hands of the people?" the question put into the senior missionary's mind an idea to open up a Christian bookstore, which he did.

Now, during your two years as a language student, you get no assignment of work, but you are asked to do little tasks here and there. So as a student, I was asked to help him in that ministry. It became his ministry, and right now that store has become one of the leading bookstores in India. Actually, it is a chain of bookstores.

When we finished language study and took an assignment, I was a missionary myself. At that point I could make some decisions and reach out in ministry. It was a small boarding school we were assigned to, and Joyce can tell about the academics of the school, because that was the area in which she was in control.

I was business manager of the school and also looked after a small church, ten or twelve miles away. But my heart, my desire, was to get the Word of God to the nation of India. Because the Bible and Christian books had such an important part in my own life, I figured that everybody should have a Bible and Christian books, books written by godly people, because they're so important.

The school assignment was a full-time job as far as the mission was concerned, but I also wanted to do Scripture distribution. So I went into the bazaar. By this time we knew the language. In the bazaar is where the vision came for the burden that was already existing within my being.

One of the first things I did was to load my shoulder bag with Gospels and New Testaments and go down into the village bazaar. Peddapalli was a small village, actually on the outskirts of a jungle area. There was a jungle very close by. There were no roads really, just dirt paths through the village, and as I was going through, I saw what would be the book stall area of the village. In India, all the shops selling the same kind of thing tend to be together. All the shops that sell books are together, and those that sell pots are together, and so on. So I went to the area where books are sold.

When I say bookstores, I don't mean what you may visualize. They were only little stalls sitting on the ground, burlap sacks in front of them, and some books laid out. I had my New Testaments, Bibles, which I was trying to distribute and sell. And I went to these bookshop keepers.

All of them, all the ones that I spoke to, were illiterate. They could not read the books that they were selling. They were business people, selling to make a profit. I asked them, "Do you know what's in these books?" to which they said, "No, we don't, but we sell them."

I asked, "Would you sell my books?" and they said, "Yes, if you give us the same terms as these people give."

I looked at the books he had for sale. They were in Telugu, the language that Joyce and I had studied, and so I knew what the content was. It was all communist literature, attractively done, well written, and at a very affordable price. I asked the man, "On what terms do you get these books?" He said they got them on consignment. They didn't have to invest any money. They got a quantity of books. When they sold them, they paid 50% to the people who supplied them and kept 50%. That was a terrific deal. They said, "If you give us the same deal, we'll do it."

At that point in time, no mission groups and no Christian bookstores in India were doing that, to my knowledge. They were giving a maximum 10% discount and requiring payment before the seller got the books. So the Communists had outwitted the whole of the Christian society in getting their literature into the hands of the people. I learned a good lesson there. I learned a lesson in marketing, a very effective technique of marketing, of getting the Word and the books into the hands of the people.

So I turned away and I cried—now in India this is nothing

unusual, because even though there are people around you, you are isolated; you can do almost whatever you want, and nobody's going to be too worried—so I cried openly. And nobody was worried about it. Tears were running down my face, and I prayed. Usually when I pray, I pray audibly, and I think I was praying audibly, but I'm not sure. I prayed, "God, this is a method that the Communists have, and we certainly can do that. I want your Word into every home in India, and I'm going to get it into the hands of the people, at a price that they can afford."

And that's where India Bible Literature was born. It wasn't called that at the time. It had no name, but that's where it was born. That's where the vision came that God gave me, to get the Word of God to every person in India. I came back and shared the vision with Joyce. It was a vision that was a total impossibility at that time. It was nothing but visionary to talk about getting the Word of God into every home in India, because at that time the Christian bookstores' shelves were full with unsold Bibles and New Testaments. Few could afford to buy them, and few would want them, because they weren't attractively portrayed.

Then God said to me, "Get the New Testaments in attractive covers." We were the first to make attractive covers in India. Until that time the covers were all black. We put pictures on them, which was revolutionary. Now all New Testaments in India have pictures on them and are attractive.

Also at that time I said, "Lord, I'm going to get God's Word to the nation of India at a price that everyone can afford. When I stand before You, no one is going to be able to point the finger at me and say, 'You kept me from getting God's Word because it was too costly.' I'm going to do what the Communists are doing: get it out, not free, but get it out at an affordable price." That was during the time when we were assigned to do school work, but my heart was in the Word of God and getting it out to the nation.

DB: And you were also a full-time pastor?

Bill: Yes, the church was in Ramagundem. It was a church with engineers that were in a big government project, and I was the pastor. But in addition to doing that church and school work, I would go out on every occasion when I had the time with one or two of the schoolboys. We would go to villages in the area around there, walking ten or twelve miles in different directions, going house to house in the villages, trying to get the Word of God into the homes. I was trying to do something with the vision that God had given to me.

DB: About what percentage of the people of India, at that time, do you believe had ever seen a Bible?

Joyce: Perhaps five percent.

Bill: Yes, at that time I would say it would be a very low percentage. Even ten years after the time that I'm speaking of, I spoke to leaders of India who came to my office — by that time I had an office — and said, "There are so many people that have never seen a Bible in their lives. We are praying for God to open up this country, that His Word will get into every home." They had been contacting thousands of homes that had not received, even ten years later, a single copy of any portion of the Word of God in any form. So I would say, at that time, a very low percentage.

DB: And twenty-five years later?

Bill: About twenty-five years, about the year 1975, was when the Word of God started to get into the homes of the people. In the early '70s we had been asked to take over as director of the World Home Bible League in India. When we began, it was a struggle to distribute a few thousand, but soon it was getting up to around 30,000 to 100,000 pieces per year. That year, 1975, was the beginning of the opening of the floodgates of getting the Word of God to the nation.

DB: And now, in 1999, it's in the tens of millions?

Bill: Yes: 70,000 pieces per working day, distributed through our five offices.

DB: I understand that none of this is free distribution. Is it true that every one of those 70,000 pieces is paid for by the people who get them?

Bill: That's right, and this is important. We never offered Bibles or Scripture portions for nothing. That was a lesson I learned very early. I don't know whether I learned this before I went to India or not, but I learned very early that free distribution is not the best stewardship of the resources that we have. I'm not condemning organizations or missions or individuals that may have a commission from God to give literature out freely. If that's their commission under God, fine, but for me it was not a good stewardship of the limited resources that we had.

DB: How did you come to that conviction?

Bill: There were several reasons. The first, which I saw very early, was that the books, booklets, and tracts that were given out free in India were taken in large quantities and sold as waste paper to the markets, where they were used as wrapping paper. Merchants were getting cheap wrapping paper, which was costly to the church.

Now, some people were saved through those wrapping papers, but to me, that was not good stewardship. I saw Bibles torn, pages torn, to wrap things in the bazaar—peanuts, whatever people were buying. So I saw quickly that probably fifty percent or more of the free books and tracts were never read. They were sold in the markets for waste paper, because paper is valuable in India.

The only way to be sure people read something in India is if they give something for it, showing that they want it. So we are putting Christian literature into the hands of people who want it; they're not taking it just because they're going to get something free.

The second reason that we ask them to pay is that it maintains the dignity of the person. We're showing them respect. Our approach to them is: "We're not trying to impose upon you something that you don't want, but we're offering you something that's good and valuable for you, worth your giving something for."

It didn't take me long over there to discover that if the people of India see something they consider to be of value, they are willing to pay for it, no matter how poor they are.

Now, they may pay in goods. In other words, I got many an egg for three Gospels. There was a barter system. They gave me an egg, I gave them a couple of Gospels. They gave me a handful of rice, I gave them a couple of booklets. So I don't mean that we always charged money. My principle was: Don't ask them to give more than they're able to, but do not give them something that they can resell, for then it becomes of no value to them.

Then, there was a third reason that just happened to work out, without my having thought about it at all. The fact that we were not giving out Scriptures free protected me from government criticism that we were proselytizing! I could truly say I proselytized no one, because I had given them nothing free. They bought it! How could the government accuse us if the people want it? If they don't want it, they don't buy it. And so that was that.

So the principle of charging for the Scriptures was economically good for us, it guaranteed that the people were getting something that they wanted and would read, and it turned out, without my realizing it, to protect us from government accusations. Now I hadn't all those reasons in mind when I did this, but it's turned out that these have been good reasons why we did this. My first reason was to ensure that it was read; that was my main reason, and because I felt that in offering the Scripture we were offering something of great value.

Bill Teate: And it wouldn't be torn up.

Bill: I could tell many stories to show how this worked out well, but I'll just tell one. We had a bookstore up in Bihar, in northeast India. The Communists controlled the government in that state. We had a bookstore up there, and one day an illiterate man whose son was the leader of the communist youth corps came in. His son was literate, in charge of all these communist youth.

When this man came in, he saw a very attractive looking book at a good price, and he bought it. He didn't know what he was buying; he was illiterate. He only knew he was buying a good book, with a lovely cover, at a good price. He assumed it was communist, because that's how they sell their books — with attractive covers. It was actually one of our New Testaments. We had put nice covers on them and put them out at a price equivalent to the communist books, so he wasn't able to discern what was what. He bought that book.

He took it home, not knowing what he had. When he showed it to his son, his son said, "Do you know what this is?" And the father said, "No, it's a book for you to read. Isn't it one of our books?" And he said, "No, it isn't, it's one of those Christian books!"

Now, if he had gotten that free, it would have been torn up and thrown in the fire. But he didn't get it for free; he had paid for it, so it was put on the table. He wouldn't throw it away, because he paid for it. As a result of the book being put on the table because it was paid for, the son read that New Testament. The son became a Christian, and we have one of the most dynamic churches today in that area through the reading of that New Testament.

So there is that principle at work. A free New Testament would have been destroyed. A bought New Testament not only brought a communist leader to Christ, but then he brought many of his young people to the Lord, and that's why it became a dynamic church.

DB: What a beautiful story! I'm wondering, though, how you managed to sell Bibles, or New Testaments, to people who did know how to read — people who would know what they had in their hands, but were not Christian. How did you persuade them to buy?

Bill: Well, that's a good question, Don. What motivation was used to get the people to buy the Scriptures? To my knowledge, I did not approach this with any kind of preconceived sales pitch, or idea of how to do it. All I wanted to do was to get the Word of God into the homes of people, and to do it in such a way that it would be read. I really had no pitch. As I look back, the real answer to that question is—and I'm not trying to be sort of frivolous by pushing it aside—that God opened the door. That's not sort of trying to be very religious or anything. I'm being honest. I worked my head off in the fifties and sixties. We distributed a few dozen a week maximum, hundreds of people said no. I had no policy for promotion.

DB: Were you saying, "This is the Word of God"?

Bill: I went and knocked on doors—actually many of the village houses had no door—but I went up to the house, the person came out, and I said, "Here's a good book." I didn't say this is the Bible or New Testament or anything like that. I said "Here's a great book that will help you in your life."

But they usually knew what we were talking about. "Oh, that's one of those Christian books. No."

We heard no a lot, and at times we had the door slammed in our faces, if there was a door. Sometimes we were verbally abused. Many didn't want it at that time, in the fifties and sixties.

It was very hard. I do not know what the explanation is. All I know is that in the fifties and sixties we worked our heads off and got very little Scripture out. But in the seventies, particularly in the mid-seventies, things changed. This was a big part of how the vision developed. In the mid-seventies it seemed that God opened the doors, and we would go to the houses, and the people would take everything that we could offer them.

Now, that was not our salesmanship. It was just that something happened in India. And, within five years after that we didn't have to go to the villages; they were coming to us, pleading to get the Word. That's why we had that spectacular distribution growth, from 3,000 a year, to 5,000 a year, to 50,000, to 500,000, and now to over twenty million. Today it's 70,000 each working day. And that's why, I mean, that wasn't any salesmanship. That was God, opening a door. And as God opened the door, then we saw the growth. That's how the vision grew in those first twenty-five years.

It started with the burden I felt as a language student. Then that vision in that little town of Peddapalli just after we finished our language studies was very significant, very definite, very clear, very focused, as to what God wanted me to do with the rest of my life. I had no doubt when I left that village street. This is what God wants me to do. So I would call that a significant day. That was a day of tears; there wasn't a blinding vision, but there certainly was a strong inward voice and conviction.

DB: And what is your vision now?

Bill: That every home in India would receive at least a portion of the Word of God. We know this is no longer an impossible dream.

## Chapter 4
# An Irish Boy

**DB:** You two are a part of this story I have never heard about. I have heard something of the miracles God has done in India. I'm very eager to hear about the miracles behind those miracles—the miracles of how God called you two, how He prepared you, and how He brought you together.

**Bill:** Joyce will be the one to do that. She can summarize it faster and probably more accurately. You put that in the book.

**DB:** What? That she's more accurate?

**Bill:** You can say faster, but don't say more accurate!

**Joyce:** The fact is, if you're more accurate, you can do it faster. You don't have room to go all over the place.

**Bill:** Well, to answer your questions would be going to the beginning of the ministry, which is what you're focusing on.

**DB:** Right. You were born in Ireland?

**Bill:** I don't mean where I was born; that would not be the beginning. I mean our coming together. That was the beginning of the ministry. But, yes, I was born in Ireland. I went from Belfast to India, and then from India to America, so my introduction to America was via India. My first furlough was my first visit to America.

**DB:** Did you two meet in India?

**Joyce:** No, in England. I was born in Plainfield, New Jersey. Most of my childhood was in Pennsylvania: Allentown, then Wilkes-Barre, in the area up around there, and then down to York. But it was in York that I came to know the Lord Jesus.

**DB:** I am very eager to hear both stories, but we have to begin with one. Bill, may I start with you?

**Bill:** Well, of course. I was born in Belfast and was brought up in that area. We lived in a working class area. On one of our furloughs, Joyce and I went to visit an area in Belfast like that. They had demolished all of the houses in which we lived, and then restored one, as a monument, to show the living conditions of the generation that has passed, how they lived. As Joyce and I went through it, we were amazed at how a family—my father and mother and her father and my two sisters and I—could all live in such a small, confined house. It was a very small house, and that was where I was brought up, where I was born.

Joyce: They called that Sandy Row, didn't they?

Bill: Yes, an area of Belfast called Sandy Row. The house was two stories, but the bottom was just a living room and dining room with a small kitchen just off, so it was really just one room downstairs. Then upstairs, one bedroom you might call the master bedroom, but in terms of bedrooms today would be a small bedroom, and then a smaller bedroom. That was it. So it was a very small area.

Joyce: A third of the size of a hotel room.

DB: How did you fit?

Bill: There were, I don't know. That is almost like a miracle. We just were…

DB: Your parents were in one room?

Bill: My grandfather was in one room. He had been wounded in the First World War and had one leg, a wooden leg, when he came out of that World War. I frequently slept with him. And somehow or other, in that other bedroom, all of us slept.

DB: Your father and mother and the children?

Bill: My father and mother and my two sisters and myself. We all slept in the other room. That's how we were brought up. My mother worked all of her life. My father worked when he could get it, but we were going through the Depression era, when very often, my father couldn't get work. He was trained in a trade that had almost disappeared in Ireland, as a linen lapper, which is a specialized trade of getting the linen and wrapping it a certain way. That's what he was, but he couldn't get into that since the linen mills were closing because of the Depression, and so he was just looking for daily work. Very often he couldn't even find that.

DB: You probably had to go to work pretty young?

Bill: I did. I went to work before I was fourteen, and then I would study in the evenings. I always had a desire to advance my education, and my parents would have liked that also, but we never had the money. They didn't have money, and we didn't have the resources for me to go to school or to college. But I worked during the day and went to evening college, which was given free of cost to those that came from our area, to all those that were poor.

So I basically grew up in a poor, working-class community. But it was a working community, not a community of taking. We had dignity in every one of our families. We were determined that we would work and earn. In other words, we weren't ever in any kind of government or social program. I don't remember us getting anything, or my parents ever getting, or expecting, or even wanting to get anything like that.

DB: There was a strong ethic against taking charity?

Bill: Oh yes, there was. Even though I would often have just a piece of bread and butter without jam, or a piece of bread and jam without butter for a meal—we couldn't have both, that was the extent of our poverty—we were willing to do that rather than to take charity and eat. Of course, I worked as soon as I could get into work. So my whole upbringing was, as I reflect on it, one of dignity.

I did not feel poor. In retrospect, I see that I am talking about poverty, but my parents, my mother, did not make us feel that we were poor. I didn't feel that we were on a poverty level. I felt that we were on a pretty good level, even though there were times when our whole family were going hungry, but we just sort of felt that was the normal way, I guess, of growing up.

But it did mean that I went to work at a very early age,

when I was fourteen. My Dad was in the army at that time. Then after the war, he was not able to get work, and I felt a responsibility in terms of wanting to earn a living.

We come from a different generation. But the fact is that in our generation, the generation in which I lived as a teenager, we worked. And I gave everything I earned to my parents. In my eyes it wasn't my money. I was working, and I gave it all to my mother. Then my mother gave me back my spending allowance out of what I gave her— which is a different philosophy from what young people live by today. But that's the way we lived. That was the normal thing; I wasn't doing anything heroic or out of the ordinary. I was doing what was, as far as I was concerned, the right, normal, natural thing to do, to give all of my money to my parents.

DB: And your father was in World War II?

Bill: He was in World War II and then, after that, found it hard to get work, and that's when we were really suffering. That was in 1945 and 1946. He was getting various jobs, and that's when I was a teenager, and that's when I was going through all of what we were going through. But all of this helped me. I think it was a part of the formation within my life, of valuing whatever resources God gives to us, however much or little. At that time it was little; and I valued the little. I believe God uses such things to train us. Because He trains you in the little, then He can trust you more and more and more. And, of course, that's where we are now, where we're relatively well off, even though others looking at us think we're still relatively poor. It depends through whose eyes you're looking. We feel we're well off, but others feel, well, they say, "You're not so well off." But in terms of what God has given us and the resources we have, we feel we are.

And it was in the midst of that time that God saved me, just before I was fifteen.

# Chapter 5

# God Saved Me

**D**B: How old were you when that happened?

Bill: In February I was saved, and my birthday was in May. So, the February of my fourteenth year God saved me.

DB: You were not brought up a Christian?

Bill: Both my parents were not Christian in the sense that we would define Christians. They were Protestant, but my dad was not even a church-going man. He never went to church. He did not speak against the church; he was a quiet person who did not condemn. The church was not spoken against, as it was in many families.

DB: You never had family worship at home?

Bill: Never had family worship at home, except with my mother. She was more religious than my dad, and she did bring me to a mission hall every Sunday night. It was a place for women who did not have the clothes to go to church. In those days, you had to have the hat, you had to have the proper dress, to go to a church. And these women did not have that. This mission hall, which was in our area, would take them as they were, no hats and with clothes, well, clothes that were clean and not ripped, but not stylish or dressy. My mother took me every Sunday night to that mission hall.

So in that way I was exposed to the Gospel from my youth, even though my mother was not a committed Christian at that time. But she did take me to the mission hall where we heard the Gospel.

And, too, I had something within my own heart as a teenager. Just prior to my teens, I read a lot. I read everything that I could get from the libraries, I was in the library, and I would take half a dozen books out, read them in a week and bring them back. I read a lot. I just liked reading. Of course, there was no TV.

DB: Had you read the Bible?

Bill: We were taught the Bible in school. This is a very interesting thing. In all the schools in Ireland when I went to school, Bible was a compulsory subject, because of the Church of Ireland. The Church of Ireland demanded that all government schools, every school in North Ireland, had to have Bible class, one hour per day. And that was taught by the priest of our diocese. He happened to be the minister of the church of which I was a member. We were all within that church. So he would come.

DB: Not Roman Catholic?

Bill: No, it was Anglican, the Church of Ireland, high Anglican. We called the ministers priests. That's what they called them there. This particular priest was a rank liberal. Of course, I didn't know that as a kid, but afterwards I learned this. He was really very liberal—did not believe the Bible, did not believe in anything. But because he was so liberal, he did not know what to teach to these kids. So he would come in every morning, as I remember it, and he would just give us a passage of Scripture and say, "Memorize that." And the examinations were just writing back what we had memorized. Now that was beautiful for me, because all those years God was implanting in my mind all this Scripture I had to memorize.

So when God saved me, that was very quickly quickened within my life. I was saved, as I said, just three months before my fifteenth birthday. I was preaching Gospel messages before I was fifteen. Within two weeks after my salvation, God quickened all this memorization so that I could get up and expound the Word, which had been instilled into my life. It's just beautiful the way God did that. It was like going to a five-year memorization class in Bible, because that's all this priest knew to do. His tests were writing out the references he asked for, and every mistake was one mark off. The more accurately you gave it back, the more marks you got. Naturally, I wanted to pass, as everyone else did, so we had to memorize.

DB: In those days, children wanted to pass!

Bill: In that day, we did. So God saved me.

DB: Was it through an evangelist?

Bill: It was actually through my own desires. There was an implantation in my life that there was something more to life than what I was getting.

I didn't know it at the time, but in looking back I see that my dad was a compulsive gambler, which made our family suffer some. And I was going in his footsteps. Apart from the grace of God, I think that I would have become a compulsive gambler. Before God saved me, I was gambling. Not the way my dad was, but any way I could, through slot machines and all that.

I was into gambling as much as I could. And I was starting to steal from my employer when I was fourteen, in order to gamble. I was working for a partnership, McKinney and Hamilton. I worked with McKinney, and McKinney would give me three or four pounds sterling, which was a large amount at that time. He gave that to me as money to spend for him. He would send me out to get a pack of cigarettes, a pound of sausages, three pounds of meat, or whatever. I would just spend that money and then come back and say, "I need more." Then he would give it to me, and then, "I need more," and he would give it to me. He wasn't even asking for receipts, and I was taking that money.

But even though I was taking it, I was very meticulous in my stealing. I recorded everything that I had stolen and everything that I lost in gambling. I was building up an account. And I hoped, I kept telling myself, "One of these days I'm going to make more and give this back." I mean, I was still basically honest, even though I was stealing. But I was getting deeper. That's what happens when you're gambling. I was getting deeper into it. And that's why I say, apart from the grace of God, I could have easily become a compulsive gambler, like my father.

It was at that time that there was an uneasiness in my whole spirit, along with a friend of mine who was a bad boy. I was a good boy. I lived a good life. I didn't smoke or drink. I wasn't into what were drugs in those days. I wasn't into bad habits, and I didn't go with women. A lot of my companions did.

There was one boy who was particularly bad. He lived on the opposite side of our street. He was about two years older than I was. God saved him, and he had a wonderful transformation of life. Everybody on the street talked about it. He was about sixteen or seventeen years old at the time, and he was bad, like a drug dealer of today. But God completely transformed him, and he then started witnessing to me. "Will you come with me to the meetings?"

I said, "Well, sometime."

Then he asked me on a Friday night—they had prayer meetings then—he said, "Bill, will you come with me to the prayer meeting tonight?" And I said, "Maybe." But I meant, "Never."

For a couple of months, God had been dealing with me in my life, you know, making me completely dissatisfied. That Friday night I went to a place where I gambled. As I recall, I'm not really sure how accurate this is, but to my knowledge, I didn't gamble that night. I remember standing in the middle of that place, people all around me, and I was struggling with God, saying, "God, if this is all that there is in life, I wish that You would just let me go. What's the sense? Am I going to just live my life, having money, gambling, losing money, gambling, sleeping, eating, gambling? What purpose? Why live?" And as I was standing on that floor, as I recall, He had appeared to my eyes, and I said, "God, I want more. I want life, if there is such a thing."

And I left that place. It was about an hour after I had gone in. I thought I was there only a minute or two, but apparently

I'd been struggling for about an hour in the midst of that gambling pit. I came running home, went over to my friend, and said, "I'll go to the prayer meeting with you."

At the next meeting, an older man greeted me, and he said, "Well, Billy, nice to see you. Why have you come?" I said, "I've come to get saved." I mean, I went there for that purpose. No one was preaching. And he said, "Well, okay, we can do that!" He led me through to the Lord. I accepted the Lord that night. And it was a real transformation of life. My life was changed.

I felt it. I was walking on cloud nine, or whatever the cloud is that you get onto. I was walking on cloud nine when I came home. My mother even said, "What's the matter with you? What's happened to you tonight?" I said, "I went up to Immanuel Mission and accepted the Lord." It was the same mission that my mother brought me to on Sunday nights; they had a Friday night prayer meeting. She was happy. She was not a Christian, but she was delighted. She said, "Well, that's good."

That was the time, of course, that I had to pay back what I had stolen. On Sunday I met with the believers in the hall. I said, "I've got a big problem." They said, "You're just a new believer." I said, "Yes, but I've got a big one." And I told them what the problem was. I said, "I stole this money. I know how much it is." Of course, I had it recorded. And I said, "I've got to replace it—tomorrow morning—to my boss. I've got to tell him." Now, no one told me I had to do that; but I just knew that's what I had to do. And I said, "Pray."

That Sunday night, my Dad, who was in the army, came home on a special leave, a six-hour leave or something, because he was being shipped over to Italy.

DB: Unexpectedly?

Bill: Unexpectedly. He didn't know then he was being shipped there. But he came home, and he said, "I'm being shipped abroad; I don't know where. I've got a three- or four-hour leave." He was stationed in Belfast. He came to me and gave me a gift, more than he had ever given me in his life.

He said, "Bill," he said, "You're the man of the house now.

You look after the house." He said, "I'm going." He said, "What will happen, I don't know." Of course, none of us knew. But he said, "You're the man of the house now. Here," and he gave me more money than he had ever given me in his life. That money was the amount of money that I needed to pay back this debt, but he knew nothing about the debt.

So I had the money. I came to the Lord, and I said, "God, I said the prayer, and now I have the money!" I said, "Now I'm going to have to hand this money back. I may be dismissed." Jobs weren't easy to find. We needed the job; I mean, I needed the job. My family needed it. And I said, "But I'm willing to trust You, God. If the boss dismisses me, I'll look somewhere else." And I expected the boss to dismiss me. So I told him the next morning, Monday morning. I said, "Sir, I've got something to tell you."

He asked, "What?"

I said, "I've been stealing from you."

He said, "What?!"

I told him what I had done, showed him the account.

He said, "What, are you cracked?"

And I said, "But I want to tell you, I've got the money, I've got it now, and I'm paying you back. Here it is. Sir, please take this responsibility from me, and give it to someone else."

He said, "Well, no, now, what's happened to you? Are you one of these born-again freaks, now?"

"That's right, that's what's happened to me. That's why I did this."

"Oh," he said, "Well, you'll be poor all your life."

I said, "Maybe I will."

But he didn't dismiss me. In fact, he started to give me a promotion, bring me into a higher position, which was unexpected. But there again, you know God.

A year later, God challenged me to complete commitment of life to Him, unreservedly, because I'd been working that year with a reservation in my heart. That reservation was, "God, I'll serve you for the rest of my life, but not anywhere else but here in Ireland—nowhere else. I like this place. I don't want to be challenged to go abroad." And I wouldn't listen to a missionary all that year.

I was always away preaching somewhere when a missionary came, until a year later, when God challenged me. That was at a meeting of young people, and that was a real challenge. I mean, I was in a sweat, and I was really making a total, absolute, no reservations commitment to God. And that, for me, was very hard. It was one of the hardest things I've ever done as a Christian.

I felt, "Boy, that was it." There's where I made the commitment that if there was anything more, I would do it. "What more can I do? What more do I need to do?" And that's what I did, just before my sixteenth birthday. This happened to be again in a February, so it was almost the first year anniversary of my conversion when I committed totally to God.

From that point on, God led me and directed me to the place where I would come to India.

# Chapter 6

# Training

**D**B: What about your schooling?

Bill: I didn't get into my education before, but if you want that now, I will.

Schooling was another step. After I made this commitment unreservedly to God, then through various ways, of course, I started listening to missionaries, reading mission books, and looking into the needs of the world, as William Carey did. I wasn't copying William Carey at that time. I hadn't heard of him, didn't know about him.

I started to read of what God was doing in different areas of the world, the needs of the world, getting statistics and information. Through all of this, I was opening my life to the world and letting God lead, whether it would be Ireland or whether it would be somewhere else.

It became very evident then that God was leading me into somewhere as a missionary into some foreign country. While this was happening, I knew that I had to get my Bible training. There were several schools in Great Britain, and one of the best at that time was the one in Glasgow, which was called the Bible Training Institute. It's now called Glasgow Bible College. That was one of the best in Great Britain.

Joyce: Didn't they call that the "Moody of Britain"?

Bill: Yes. It was founded by D. L. Moody, so it was like Moody Bible Institute in America. But in Great Britain, among all the Bible schools, it was counted as one of the best and one of the more costly.

I could have found cheaper schools in Belfast, less expensive ones in London, in Bristol, or in different parts of Great

Britain. But the one in Glasgow, of course, if I had had the choice, would have been the one that I would have chosen. Again, I was doing the research. I was reading about Bible schools, Bible colleges—getting to know what was available.

At that time, I was working in the same mission where my mother used to take me. I was doing the preaching and in charge of children's meetings, doing several meetings and various activities within the mission. A very rich businessman in Belfast had built the mission. He had Parkinson's disease at the time when we were working there. He was still active, but he couldn't preach. But he was always at the meetings.

Then one Sunday night, out of the blue, he came to me and said, "Billy, are you thinking of going to Bible school?" They all had known of my commitment and where I was. I said, "Yes, I am." He said, "Well, why don't you write to BTI?" He chose this one, the one that I would have chosen. He said, "Why don't you write to them and see what they say?" I said, "Okay." And he said, "When they tell you, let me know."

So I wrote to them, and they sent me back an application. I sent in the application, and in a very short time they accepted me. They wrote, "You're accepted; you can start in September." I don't know what month we were in—maybe July, maybe August. But it wasn't too long before the time I was to start.

I went back to this businessman, and he said, "Well, what's happened?" I said, "I've been accepted." He said, "Oh? For when?" I said, "I can start in September." He said, "What are you going to do?" I said, "I'm not really sure," which I wasn't. He said, "Well, this is Sunday night. Come to my office tomorrow morning."

I knew where his office was, even though I'd never been there before. But I went to his office next morning. I had never been in a big plush office like that in my life. For me, it was overwhelming. He ushered me inside and said, "Okay, here." And he handed me a wad of bills, which was more than over-whelming. It was more money than I had ever had in my hands at one time.

And I looked at it, and I said, "What's this?"

He said, "That's to buy your new suits and everything you need, including your boat ticket, to go to Glasgow to BTI." And I was overwhelmed. I mean, it was totally, absolutely unexpected. I never knew things like that happened, especially to me. I was thinking of working for ten years trying to save up something, and then ultimately going to college.

So I said, "Okay." I said, "Lord, this is terrific! Thank you, God!" I went out, of course, and bought the suits, because he asked to see them. He said, "I want this. This is for you to buy suits." He knew that I would probably give the money away, and he said, "I don't want that to happen." So I bought them, got my ticket, and went.

There I was, studying happily, and after about a month—this happened in these Bible schools—a notice went up on the boards. The notice read: "All students who have not paid their fees, please report to the business office with your suitcases packed to leave." That was fair enough. I mean, they couldn't keep feeding us, teaching us, if we hadn't paid our fees. I hadn't paid a penny, because my sponsor had given me just enough for me to get there and to spend, so I had no money.

I thought, "God, what do I do?" The thought came to me that it was going to come in the mail, and I prayed, "Lord, you're going to send this." Up to the last day, when I got a letter, somebody would write, "We're praying for you, Billy, God bless you." And I think, "Yeah, you may be praying, but where's the money? I need the money now, and I don't have a penny in any pocket. God, this is ridiculous. Where am I going to go? What am I going to do?"

Since the funds didn't come, I said, "Well, I can't stay here then. I haven't paid." So I did what we were told, and I packed. It was no big deal packing. I mean, I only had one small suitcase with a couple of shirts, a suit. It wasn't too much to pack. So I had the suitcase packed, as we were told. I went down to the business office—I left the suitcase in my room—to sign out or whatever I had to do.

I went in to see the business manager, and he said, "Who are you?"

I said, "Scott. Billy Scott from Belfast."

And he said, "What is it?"

I said, "The notice was up. This is the last day, and I'm ready to go."

He said, "Wait a minute." He went over into his records, pulled them out, and said, "You don't need to go."

I asked, "What do you mean, I don't need to go?"

He said, "Your fees have been paid for the entire year."

I responded, "What?"

He asked, "Why didn't you come before?"

I said, "Because I had nothing to pay you. I couldn't come."

He said, "If you had come before, we would have told you."

I asked, "Why didn't you tell me first?"

He said, "Well, we were expecting you to come in."

Then I asked, "What do you mean, it's paid?"

He said, "Mr. Downham (the businessman) has prepaid your first year, totally."

I said, "Oh, thanks a lot."

Of course, I thanked Mr. Downham. He died that year while I was there. Then I got a notice in the mail from a lawyer that read, "You are named in the will of Mr. Downham." I'd never been named in the will of anybody before.

I said, "Oh boy, I'm named in the will." He, in his will, provided education not only for the next year, but for all further ongoing education that I needed, which I did.

DB: Amazing!

Bill: God did that. And that's the story. So that set me on the course where I knew that I could completely trust God. Even when I was up against a wall, I knew I could trust Him.

This was the beginning of my part in the ministry. I know Joyce has just as exciting a beginning. That gets us to the point where we would be going to India soon.

## Chapter 7
# The Call to India

**D**B: How many years did you go to BTI?

    Bill: That was a two-year course. I could have done a three-year program, but I chose not to do the third, and then I went to a secular college rather than spend the money on repeating courses.

DB: Where did you go for a secular college?

Bill: In Belfast, in my hometown. It was Renshaw College. that's another story. Everything leads into other stories! I don't know where we stop in these. But that's another story.

For a year I went to a college in Belfast that was called Renshaw College. Then I went to do a course in what we call matriculation. I was also taking a course with the London Chamber of Commerce. I was combining a commerce and accounting course with academic preparation for a college degree. But even after I had finished that course, and it took a year, I still wasn't sure when God would open up the way for me to get to India.

DB: You had already settled on India?

Bill: I had already by that time settled on India.

Joyce: And that was a struggle also?

Bill: That was a struggle, too, but that's another story.

Joyce: The story there is significant in the sense that, the night that he was really challenged, all his other buddies kept saying, "C'mon, Bill, let's go, the meeting's over." But he would not leave. He just held on to the pew in front of him in a cold sweat, because he was going through such a struggle as to whether he would say yes to India and the mission field, or whether he would say no. His buddies were saying, "C'mon," and he kept holding on to the pew.

Bill: I didn't know until afterwards that the missionary that spoke that night was a missionary from India. I had temporarily forgotten that; I met her years later. But, as Joyce said, that night there were young fellows with me. You see, we had a team of young people, including a number of them I had led to the Lord.

I was the preacher, as I told you, and they sort of looked to me as the preacher and teacher. I had led these young fellows to the Lord, and then we had evangelized our whole working class area, thousands of homes. We had gone from home to home. We had made a commitment to God and said, "There won't be one person in this whole area that will be able to stand before God and say 'I never heard the Gospel.' We will tell everybody."

So we spent months going to every house, talking to them about Jesus. Some of them threw us out, but most of them didn't. We were kids, so they listened. They said, "Okay, better for these young people to be here talking about Jesus than doing something else." Usually they said, "No, we don't want you inside," so we just stood outside the house and preached the Gospel so they could hear it. You were allowed to do that in those days. We would have an open-air meeting, and I would preach for twenty minutes. So they figured, "If we don't let them in, we're going to get preached to anyway, so we'd better let them in." These were the same fellows who were with me.

DB: And that's the year that you were fifteen?

Bill: It was just before my sixteenth birthday. We had evangelized our whole area; that was the commitment that we had made to God. We'd done it. Out of that, these were the group of young men whom I had basically led to the Lord. My other companions had also led some to the Lord. But every time we went to a meeting, people would go from our meeting to some other activity, and our activity would always be to the fish and chip shop. There was a very good fish and chip shop in our area, and we would go and have fish and chips. Sometimes we would share plates together, because we didn't always have enough money. But we had fish and chips.

So that's what they were anxious for, because the fish and chip shop was going to close if we didn't leave soon. They were saying, "C'mon! We're going to be too late." I said, "Go and have your fish and chips, but I can't. This is not just something casual, something where I just throw my name in. I'm struggling, and I want to make this definite. It's either going to be a 'yes' or a 'no' to God in terms of where He wants me to serve Him." That's the struggle Joyce was talking about. That's when I made the commitment. I said, "Okay, God, I will commit to go anywhere."

DB: And the call specifically to India, when was that?

Bill: It grew from that. Apparently that missionary had put into my heart something about India, but I wasn't aware of it in my conscious mind. I didn't even know who it was. But I think that's where the seed of India was implanted within my being. And then, of course, through research and study, God definitely showed me. He said, "Bill,…" and I knew. You just come to that point that you know that you know that this is what God wants. It wasn't that I heard a voice or that I was pushed, but I just knew that I knew that it was India. Originally I had settled on two countries, either Egypt or India, and I knew it would be one of them. Then Egypt was eliminated, and I knew that I knew that it was India, and India for life.

Here's an odd thing. Some time later I met that missionary, not knowing it was the same person. We were talking about my commitment to India, and she asked, "Where did you make this commitment?" I told her. Then she asked, "Do you know who the missions speaker was that night?" I said, "No, I don't remember." You see, all through the message I was struggling internally. I don't think I was hearing clearly, but subconsciously it must have been going in. I was struggling internally with God. So I said, "No, I really don't remember." She said, "Do you remember what country that missionary was from?" I said, "No, I don't." She said, "I was that missionary." I said, "So I heard about India that night?" She said, "Yes, I was the speaker that night."

DB: Do you remember her name?

Bill: I should know it; I can see her face, but I can't get the name. She was a CIGM missionary.

DB: What is CIGM?

Bill: Ceylon and India General Mission was the name then.

Joyce: We used to say CIGM stood for "Come In and Get Married" mission.

Bill: That would have been a big sacrifice for me at that time! A big price to pay! That was a call that didn't work until I got to India.

DB: And when did you leave for India?

Bill: Well, I didn't know how long I had to wait between that and going to India. It might have been a year, it might have been two. I knew I would go as soon as I could get accommodations on a boat. In those days you went by boat, and at that time the boats were all booked one, two, three, four years ahead of time. You couldn't just go down and say I want a ticket for tomorrow, as you can on air flights. They'd say, "You're number 54 on the waiting list."

I was on the waiting list; I don't know what number I was, but I got on that waiting list. Normally it would take about two years before the number I was on the list came up. That was how I knew I needed to do something for a year or a year and a half, maybe longer.

I tried to find a church to pastor, but none of the Baptist churches were interested. A number of them said, "Oh, yes, we'll give you a call as a pastor, but you'll have to stay." And I said, "That's not what I want. I don't want to stay. I'm going to be a missionary." They said, "Don't tell us that; we won't call you." I said, "I'm telling you that," and they wouldn't call me.

So I couldn't get into any Christian service by virtue of the fact that they knew within a year or two I'd be gone to India. Of course, I could understand that, but I was disappointed, and

I prayed, "God, why can't I get into Christian service?"

I had to try to get a secular job during that time, and I registered at the employment agency. They said, "There's a job as a cost accountant in a factory." Now I was not a cost accountant. I had done accounting up to the equivalent, as far as I understand now, of being a CPA. I had done that, but I hadn't done cost accounting. I'd taken some courses in cost accounting, but I wasn't a cost accountant. But I went to this company and applied.

This is the interesting part, now. The employment exchange gave me the address. When I went, I saw the cost accountant and the secretary of the company, and had an interview. Both of them said, "Okay, we'll see." I walked from that company to my house. It was about a half an hour's walk, and I like walking. So I walked home. When I got home, there was an envelope below in my hall, right below the door, from this company, saying, "You are hired. Report for work tomorrow." I was amazed!

That's not the end of the story. You see, what had happened in the interview was this. The cost accountant had said, "Where did you study?" I said, "Well, my last place was Renshaw College," and he said, "Oh, I'm a graduate of Renshaw." I said, "You are?" And then we got talking for about half an hour on all the good things at Renshaw. So our God just led me. I could have chosen a half a dozen other colleges, but that was the one I'd gone to, and that was part of the miracle.

When I went there to this company the next day, I saw the rest. He just opened up the office, and he said, "Well, okay." He had just been promoted to works manager. He said, "Okay, Billy" (they called me Billy in Ireland). He said, "Okay, Billy, the office is yours. You're the cost accountant. I'm the works manager from today. You're the cost accountant." I said, "I told you I know nothing about it." He said, "That's why you got the job." I said, "Why? What do you mean?" He said, "You were the only honest person that came into this office, and the secretary told me, 'If that guy is as honest as that, take him.'"

See, they had asked me at the interview. That was the one query. He had asked, "Do you know cost accounting?" I said, "No, but I can learn it, because I have this background." So when he was explaining why I was hired, he said, "You floored us! We have two or three other questions that would have determined whether you knew. Every one before you said, 'Oh, yes,' and within two questions we knew that they weren't telling the truth. But you floored us. That's why you got it." That was the job I worked at for a year, which was a good experience.

After a year, then the passage opened where I went to India, and it happened to be the same boat as a Miss Joyce Yost was traveling on. I thought, "Miss Joyce Yost! That will be some dear old missionary lady, a gray haired lady with a bun in the back of her head, and she'll look after me," because I thought that's what all the missionary ladies were like.

Joyce: They might have had the gray hair, but the one that did the looking after was me.

Bill: I thought that was what all the lady missionaries were like. Then I went to London with my friend. I saw this beautiful young girl in a red coat, chewing gum and reading American airmail. I thought, "Lord, it can't be…" Then a lady came out and said, "Oh, I want to introduce you to Miss Yost." My heart leapt, and I thought, "God! How you have changed me!"

DB: It sounds like we're getting close to the happy ending, or rather, the happy beginning, since you say the ministry really began when you and Joyce started working together in India.

Bill: I just have to add one thing first, which is very significant. When I was saved, I was the only one in our family at that time who was a born-again Christian, or whatever way you want to define it, but before I left for India my mother and two sisters accepted Christ, too. So they were believers and had been worshipping with me and praising God, and releasing me into missions, even though it was heartbreaking to my mother.

My dad was still the same when I left for India as he had

always been. We had talked together, and he had heard me preach, because I had meetings in our home. I had opened our home to bring the Gospel to people in our area. Every week we would have a meeting, and I would be the preacher. My Dad had heard me at some of those meetings, but he still was not a believer.

When I got to India, there was a cablegram from Ireland the day I arrived. It was from my brother-in-law who was a believer and married to my sister who was also a believer. The gist of the cablegram he sent was: "Bill, the first convert that you have had in going to India is your father. When you left on the boat, he came back with us and said, 'I never thought that Billy would go through with this. If he has a God like that, if he's willing to give his life in India for that God, I want to know Him.' We led your father to Christ the night that you left."

# Chapter 8

# A Pennsylvania Dutch Girl

D B: We've gotten Bill to that boat, Joyce, and we've heard what he thought when he saw you. I want to know what you thought when you saw him, but first, how did you get to that boat?

Joyce: I was born into a family where neither my mother nor my father was a Christian. Mother was a Quaker, a "birthright Quaker" as they called them. Dad was Lutheran. Neither one knew the Lord. When I was two years old, Mother accepted the Lord through the ministry of F. F. Bosworth, a well-known evangelist at that time. He had big campaigns, and the lady next door was a Christian and had invited Mother to go.

DB: This was in Pennsylvania?

Joyce: Bethlehem, Pennsylvania. I was two when mother accepted the Lord. And I had two older brothers. There were three of us born in two and a half years; my brothers and I were very close. About two years after that, Dad accepted the Lord. Shortly after that, he took on the responsibility as superintendent of the Allentown Rescue Mission, which is opposite the train station.

I was taken as a four- or five-year-old child to the nightly meetings, and I would see these derelicts and drunkards, and smell this—I can still almost smell it now—the aroma of liquor all over the room and the other aromas from these men. I felt so sorry for them, and I began to realize that the Gospel was really "rescue" for such people. But as I got older, even though I was still going to church and Sunday school, and also to the rescue mission, I made no move toward making a decision for myself.

Dad was in government work. He did a lot of moving

around, and of course we had to shift with him. So we had no anchors in one particular church. I had heard the Gospel, of course, when I was going to the meetings at the rescue mission. I remember going to the Pentecostal Holiness church as a very young girl. Later we went to a Nazarene church. It was like that. And later on a Methodist.

We were in the Wilkes-Barre area for seven years, and then we went to other towns. Finally Dad was sent to York, Pennsylvania, to work on flood control. He was working for the civilian department of the United States Army Engineers. I was going to junior high on the western side of York. We joined the Lutheran church. I went to confirmation classes and was confirmed. There was a very fine pastor there, Dr. J. B. Baker. I became very good friends with him and got interested in the church. I was sort of a leader among the young people.

Some time after that Dad had an accident, out on the roadside while he was overseeing some projects there. It meant that he could not work, and he was the only one in the family working. So our pennies dwindled down and down. There came a time where we had ten cents to spend for breakfast, ten cents to spend for lunch, and ten cents to spend for supper. I remember Mother taking cans of minced meat and putting them behind the radiators to warm them up so that she could open them and feed us.

One day in November that year, it was close to Thanksgiving time, I had gone with a couple of girl friends into a place where we high school kids hung out. I saw the boy—I don't even remember his name now—the boy with whom I had a date for Thanksgiving night. And for some reason I went over to him and said, "If you don't mind, I think I'd like to break the date for Thursday night." So he said, "Okay, we'll get together later."

When Thanksgiving Day came, I had offered to go to the Salvation Army to help serve the food to the folks who were coming to get free food, the very poor people, and I saw the Salvation Army girls who were there. They had such peaceful looks on their faces, and there was such a radiance about them. I thought to myself, "Boy, this is interesting. I don't think I look like this."

That evening Mother said, "I think we'll go up to the York Gospel Center where Rev. Ralph Boyer is tonight, and I'd like you to go along." At that point I could have said, "Oh, Mother, no." I could have made some typical teenage excuse, and Mother would not have said, "You must." But I said, "Okay." The family started ahead of me, and I realize now that I could have at any time just gone in any other direction, to my friend's home or something. But I went to the service. I did go, on my own. I walked up to the Gospel Center a mile or so away.

There I saw Mother and Dad sitting way down in front of the church, and I thought, "Why are they way down there?" They were about six rows from the front, and everybody else seemed to be in the back. I went up and sat with them, and there were two other girls sitting right down at the front there. One was the pastor's daughter, and the other was a high school girl from the congregation.

There was special music on the program; the Berg sisters from Maryland were up singing. And they were singing, "Oh, oh, He's done so much for me. Oh, oh, He's done so much for me. If I should try through all eternity, I could never tell what He's done for me." And I thought, "No, I can't say that! I can't say that! I can't say that!" And I looked at those two girls there down in the front row, and I thought, "There's something about them that is beautiful, you know. I don't have it."

The sermon was a beautiful message on Thanksgiving, a very practical one for that time. But a service with Rev. Boyer was never finished until he gave an invitation. And that night, as he gave the invitation for those who wanted to accept Christ, my hand just went up. Another thing he did every once in a while, was to come down off the platform and walk, just to see if there was somebody he saw who might be ready to move forward. He came down off of the platform and stepped in where I was, and he just put his hand out, and I just walked down to the altar.

DB: How old were you then?

Joyce: I was a junior in high school. That was the night that I fully, completely, just totally gave my life to Christ. So it was no longer just church membership or church activities. I had even started a young girl's missionary society in the Lutheran church when we were going there. The first book we ever studied happened to be about India, but I never felt I was going to India. About that time, a Lutheran missionary spoke at that church. We young girls were all inspired and named our society the Emma Johnson Missionary Society. Much later, in India, I met the woman who had been the speaker and told her my story. I believe those little things come along in your life to let you see how God is at work in all things for those who love Him, you know, Romans 8:28.

The following year, my senior year, just around Easter time I walked into the York Gospel Center—I had started going there regularly—for one of their Saturday night youth meetings. Now on the back wall they used to put up Bible verses, and when I walked in that night there was a new verse. It was Isaiah 45:22: *"Look unto me, and be ye saved, all the ends of the earth: for I am God, and there is none else."* And that seared my mind, my heart, my thoughts, almost my body. I just looked at that, and immediately the Lord said to me, "That's what I want you to do: go to the ends of the earth." I didn't expect that, that night, but that's what happened. And so I yielded to that, not knowing where or what was really involved.

In the meantime, just prior to that, during my junior year, I had dedicated my life to the Lord, to work wherever He wanted, but I wanted it to be in the laboratory. I was very interested in science—very, very interested in science. I had planned to go to Bethlehem, Pennsylvania, and, in fact, I had been accepted at the Moravian College for Women in Bethlehem and had expected to go into scientific research in cells and tissues. That was really what I wanted to do. So when this message about the ends of the earth came to me, the Lord led me to what is now Columbia International University. It used to be Columbia Bible College in Columbia, South Carolina.

The day that I left to get on the train, I had practically no money. I had $9.65 in my pocket. My mother was very upset that I was going without having it all planned and secure. Dad was still not that well, so there wasn't a lot of money. But I was sure that Columbia was where the Lord wanted me to go. Mother had even said, "Oh, well, you'll go down there and you'll fall in love with some fellow and you won't go into Christian work at all anyway," and things like that. She was not against what I was doing, but she was trying to make me see, as a young eighteen-year-old, you know, that there were other things to consider.

Well, the day I left, as I said, I had $9.65. There were about five or six of us from York all going on the same train, the Silver Meteor, down to Baltimore, and then on to Columbia. Many people came to see us off at the train, and many people pushed little envelopes into my hand as we were leaving. When the train left, after saying goodbye to all the people, I counted the money they had given to me, and with my $9.65 there was exactly $150. That's exactly what I had to have for the business office when I got there.

To help work my way through school, I got a job in a shoe store, but I soon got fired. If shoes didn't fit, I told the people so. The manager didn't like that. So I was dismissed. Then I got a job that paid fifty cents an hour, working for two ladies who were on the board of the Bible college, drawing pictures on stencils. I thought that was good money. But all during that time, gifts would come in, totally unexpectedly. They augmented what I was earning during the day.

Not long after I started my studies, the young man that was the head of our table in the dining room, Steve Zucker, said to me one day: "Joyce, I believe the Lord wants me to pay for you to go to the Student Foreign Mission Fellowship regional conference at Asheville, up at Ben Lippen."

And I said, "The Lord told you that?" I hardly knew the

Lord knew my name in that way. And he said, "Yes, I believe the Lord wants me to do that."

I got approval from the Dean of Women, Clara Walker. Of course, there were a lot of other people going, several others in the car. So she said, "Okay." I didn't know what was going to happen. We got to Ben Lippen on Friday. We had a meeting that night, and meetings during the day on Saturday. Saturday night we gathered around a beautiful stone fireplace. The logs were burning, and we had a lovely meeting. Pat Major, who was Conservative Baptist, talked about India. He was planning to go to India.

Now the only thing I remember, Don, out of that whole message was this: he said that, at that point in 1942, there were 392 million people who had never heard the name of Jesus in India, 392 million who had never heard the name of Jesus.

Just like Isaiah 45:22 had gone into my soul and my spirit, that statistic did the same thing. The Lord began to deal with me and challenge me. I said, "Lord, the war is on, and the Japanese are over there. Who wants to go to India in this situation? Lord, how? I don't see how I can go." But I began to go to the Student Foreign Mission Fellowship, to the India prayer group, every Saturday, and I began to learn many things about India.

I didn't really do anything about it, though, until I was a junior. That was two and a half years. In the spring of my junior year, it got to the point where I knew I had to say yes or no. I'd been thinking of Africa. All I ever heard as a kid was Africa, Africa, Africa, and I had known very little about India. But I got on my knees one afternoon, and I said, "Okay, Lord, if it's India, I'll go."

The very next day I got a letter from Rev. Boyer saying that the church committee had voted that for any young person who would go to the mission field from the Gospel Center, they would pay their support, monthly support, and pay their fare. The very next day!

It was like that all through my whole four years. I was

working in the dining room, working in various places, earning some money and trusting the Lord for the rest. At the end of every year I would go to the business office and say, "What is my balance for the year?"

And the business woman there, the business officer, said, "Well, Joyce, you don't owe anything."

"I don't? But I must, according to my…"

"No, everything's clear." That happened all four years.

DB: That's remarkably like Bill's school experience!

Joyce: All our lives it has been the same!

I remember once during my junior year the Dean of Women, Mrs. Clara Walker, called me down out of a class and asked me if I had money to pay for my board and room. I may have been three or four months late. And she said, "You're eating food you haven't paid for." I didn't like that, because I certainly wasn't there to eat food I didn't pay for. And she said, "Well, I'm afraid you'll have to go and pack your things and go home. You might as well go up to the trunk room and get your things."

I was on my way up to the trunk room on the open elevator — there was a wire elevator you could see out of — and I saw the Assistant Dean of Women on the steps. She said, "Oh, Joyce, wait a minute," so the person operating the elevator stopped, went back down, and she said, "I have a special delivery letter for you."

I took the letter, and I opened it, and it was from my mother. And it was a check for the exact amount that I owed for those months that I'd been eating food I hadn't paid for. The letter said, "I'm sending this on, Joyce, because this is some sort of a rebate from the insurance we had on you," or something like that, "and I'm sending it on to you." Now, what I owed was only about $30 or $40 a month at that time, because we didn't have to pay tuition. It was just for the board and room.

And so victoriously, I went back down to the Dean of Women and said, "Here." Well, she was very flabbergasted, of course. But it was God's faithfulness that I didn't have to pack up my clothes and leave in the middle of my junior year.

Bill Teate: Sometimes I think our affluence in America prevents us from really seeing God's provision.

Bill: That's right; that's true.

Joyce: Another time, in the summer just before my senior year, Dad came home from some secret Army work he had been doing during World War II. He came in and said, "I just want to tell you both," (that was mother and me), "that I've received a raise, and it is just enough, every month, to pay for Joyce's board and room." And of course, Dad could have given it to anything. He could have put it toward their own expenses, but he came and said that.

Well, of course, there were other expenses as well, you know, for books and things. But at the end of my senior year, just as we came away from the graduation ceremonies, I went to the business office, and again I said, because I knew there were things there that should be paid, "What do I owe?"

Miss Owens said, "Joyce, you don't owe anything."

And I asked, "Will you please tell me who has been paying my bills?"

She replied, "Miss Sophie Graham. Every year, she has come and asked what you had left, and she paid it."

She was a retired missionary with the Southern Presbyterians to China. She had been coming at various times and was pretty much moving around, visiting at the Bible college, and somehow or another the Lord just laid me on her heart. So every year I went home debt-free, while other people went home with bills. All they earned during the summer had to go to pay what was owed; it wasn't helping them get ready for what was ahead.

So the Lord was really tremendously faithful in all the little ways as well as the big ways, And each one of those was again a confirmation that God was with me, that I was definitely where He wanted me to be, because He was providing and making the way for me to do what I was doing.

# Chapter 9

# York Meets Belfast in London

D B: And how did you get to India?

Joyce: Well, when I graduated from Columbia in 1946, I had not yet decided what mission board to go out with. I knew I wanted to go with a mission board that worked in the villages, not in the cities. Also I felt that I needed a couple of "boot camp" years, working in Christian work here. So the first year out of Columbia I taught Bible in public schools in Tazewell, Virginia, although I had always said I would never be a teacher. No way! But the Lord had led me to take teacher training at Columbia, and I got my teaching certificate.

From Virginia I went to Erie, Pennsylvania, where I had been asked to establish a program of religious education in the Erie County public schools. This was an outreach of the Erie County Sabbath School Association, back in the days when the Bible had an accepted place in education almost everywhere.

That happened to be the year that Madeline Murray O'Hare started all the trouble about the Bible in public schools, and the Bible program in the Pennsylvania schools was cut. So I got a job teaching third grade in a public school in Baltimore—in the roughest, hardest part of the city, at Baltimore and Monroe Streets. It was just terrible.

Now the daughter of a minister had seen me at a camp where I was director, a Christian girls' recreational camp on Lake Erie. He invited me to be Director of Religious Education in his church, the First Presbyterian Church in Erie, Pennsylvania. After one year there he asked me to stay on, but I said, "No, I've got to go to India." He offered to double my salary if I stayed, but I said no. Of course, he knew I loved the Lord, you know, my heart was in the work, and that's what he wanted.

DB: Did you ever regret turning down that opportunity?

Joyce: No. I knew I was called to India. Also, it turned out that he died in November of that year, so had I stayed on at his request, he would not have been there for us to minister together.

During this time I was going back and forth to Penn Grove Christian Camp, which the York Gospel Center had taken on. Meanwhile I had been researching missions, looking for one that worked in the villages, and I had settled on the India Mission, which is now International Missions. The man who was the founder had visited Columbia a couple of times, and I asked him, "What is your work?" And he said, "It's all villages." That's what interested me. I applied and was accepted.

I had a booking on the Queen Mary to sail on the 29th of September. I had eight days layover between the arrival of the Queen Mary from New York and the sailing of the boat to India from Tilbury. When I got to England, I visited with a gal who had been doing Bible club movement work. She was from Philadelphia. She met me at the boat in Southampton and took me up to Birmingham. I had a terrific time there, about five or six days meeting a lot of Christians in that area. Then on Wednesday I came down to the China Inland Mission Home in London.

It was a kind of guest home, with a lot of rooms, almost like a hotel, but very primitive. I was in the office there, paying my bill, asking the superintendent to finish up everything for me, and she said, "Well, I don't know where Mr. Scott is. He's due in anytime." Now I had known that there was a Mr. William Scott who was coming to get on the same boat out of England, from Ireland. The mission office had informed me of that, but that was all. And so I said, "I have no information," and I just sort of let it go at that.

While I was there in the office, I saw two fellows come up and walk in the door. They introduced themselves and the superintendent lady said, "Oh, Miss Yost, I'd like to introduce you to Mr. Scott, and this is his friend Jack Hull." I turned around and said, "Hello," and went on and finished what I had to do. They got their room assignments, and this Mr. Scott and I ended up sort of going out of the office about the same time.

He said to me, "Do you know where the P & O shipping office is?"

And I said, "Yes, it's down off of Trafalgar Square."

He said, "Can you show me where that is?"

I said, "Well, I happen to be going in to meet somebody at Trafalgar Square, to the tea shop, so we can go down together."

So we met again in about another twenty minutes or so, and he said, "Well, let's go on the Underground."

I said, "No thanks, I'm not interested in the Underground. I don't like the Underground; I have somewhat of a claustrophobic thing, and I don't like the idea of going underground like that. I found my way down there by surface travel, so if you want to come on the surface, I'll show you."

And he said, "Okay, we'll go along."

So we got on the bus and the trolleys and headed down that way, and this fellow says to me, "How many pieces of luggage do you have?"

I said, "Well, I've got eighteen. How many do you have?"

"Well, I have three, plus a bike and a trunk."

"Oh," I said, "really?" Now I think that at that point he decided, "This gal's got eighteen pieces. She must have a lot of stuff. All I have is this; I should join up with her," so he could use all my household goods.

Bill: I didn't have any!

Joyce: The story goes that when people were giving Bill gifts, they wanted to give him the fish fork and the fish knife, which is so British. And somebody came to give him a couple of these so he could take them with him and he said, "Oh, no, I only want one knife and one fork. I'm alone; why would I want anything more than that?" His idea at that point was he didn't need anything more than what he might need for himself.

Anyhow, we got off the bus down at Trafalgar Square. I pointed down, and I said, "Do you see that sign coming out there?"

He said, "Yes."

I said, "Well, that's where you go."

He didn't have his ticket yet. So he had to go down there and get his ticket. And I said, "See you later." I went and had my tea date with my friend and went back to the China Inland Mission home.

Supper time came, and we were all standing around, milling around out in the hall waiting for the bell to ring for us to go into the dining room. The lady superintendent came up to me and asked, "Where's Mr. Scott?"

I said, "Well I don't know!" I was a little bit, slightly indignant. Why should I know where some man was? I didn't know him; I just happened to show him where he was going.

"Well," she said, "he hasn't come back."

I said, "Well, I don't know where he is. I left him at Trafalgar Square, and I went on and took care of my appointment and came back here, so I don't know anything about it."

And she said, "Well, I don't know what to do."

I said, "What would you usually do?"

"Well, we could wait for a few minutes."

So I said, "Well, then wait for a few minutes."

The problem was, there was a gas strike on, you know, for cooking gas, and they heated the rooms with gas, and so they didn't want to keep the stoves running longer than they had to. So I said, "Well, you just do what you feel right."

So she said, "Well, we'll wait for a few minutes."

About twenty minutes later, she said, "He hasn't come yet."

I said, "Well, I just don't know what to do. Why don't you just go on and eat?"

She said, "Okay," she rang the bell, and we all went in to eat.

By the time we ate, he still hadn't come, and she came back

to me. "Well, what will I do?"

There I was, an American, and we're so informal we would have just said he could get something in the kitchen when he got in. But I didn't know what they did, so I said, "Well, I really don't know, I think you just do whatever you feel you should do. What is your custom here?"

So we finished, she closed up the dining room, and that was it.

One of the ladies had been with me on the Queen Mary. She had been a missionary to China, and she said, "Joyce, I want you to come up to my room for a couple of minutes here after supper."

So I went up there, and she gave me a beautiful little gilt-edged, India paper, leather bound *Daily Light*. And she said, "I just want to give this to you as a remembrance of me." We had gotten to be good friends on the boat. I still have that book. It was a beautiful remembrance of that whole time. And so we had fellowship together, had prayer together, and I opened the door to go out.

Her room was sort of on a landing, after you come up a set of stairs, there's a landing, then go up this way. The door to her room was on that landing, and when we opened it, there was Bill!

He was coming up the steps, along with his friend Jack. Like a typical American woman, you know, I said, "Where have you been?"

He looked at me, his face got red, and he said, "We got lost on the Underground."

And I'm thinking, "Here this fellow was wanting me to go on the Underground with him to go down to Trafalgar Square!" I said, "What do you mean, you got lost? How do you get lost on the Underground?"

Sheepishly, he had to say, "We were reading the map backwards."

Bill: And getting on the wrong lines.

Joyce: And getting on the wrong lines. His moment of

pride was in telling us that it only cost him tuppence, two pennies more, to get out of there after all that time of hours and hours, going all over on the Underground. He must have been to every part of London it was possible to go to. I thought, "I'd better be careful with this fellow, you know."

Chapter 10
# India!

**Joyce:** Well, the day after Bill's London Underground adventure, we left and got on the boat train, heading for Tilbury. We spent eighteen days on that boat. I had learned a little bit of the Telugu language at the candidate school, so I was teaching him what I knew, and he was asking me questions. He had not been to the candidate school, so it was an opportunity to share some of the orientation that we got.

**Bill:** Yes, and that turned out to be very important later, as you will see. But in spite of all of the orientation regarding India that we had in London, when we really came to India, it was a shock.

**DB:** When was it that you got there?

**Bill:** October 28, 1950. We arrived by boat, so we arrived into a crowded, cramped dock area.

**DB:** Bombay?

**Bill:** Bombay. There were literally thousands of men working on all the boats. They called them coolies. So we just saw these, and in my first impression they reminded me of colonies of ants, constantly moving, carrying, moving, carrying. We suddenly saw the reality of what was at that time about 450 million people. Of course, now the population has greatly increased. About doubled?

**Joyce:** Yes, because in 1942 it was 392 million. That's what the Lord spoke to me about, about the 392 million. In just eight years it was up to around 450 million.

**Bill:** So many people.

**Joyce:** I had my own reaction that morning as we arrived.

The ship pulled in to Bombay about 6:00 or 6:30 in the morning. Bill was handling whatever he had left down in his stateroom, but I had finished up all my packing.

Bill: We were not yet married at that time.

Joyce: I went up to the deck as we pulled in. As the gangplanks were put down, I stood there and overlooked what was happening. Bill mentioned the people, all these coolies going in and out. When I looked down at these people, my heart broke.

Man after man, with heavy, heavy things on their backs. How they could lift them I didn't understand. Later I found out that at the place where the load was picked up, there were usually a couple of men to lift it and put it on the back of the man who was going to carry it. But at that time I just saw them going, line after line, line after line, carrying these burdens. And I started to weep as I saw this.

There were seventy-seven missionaries on that ship as it left England. Some were on their way to Australia and other places in the South Seas. Most of them were getting off at Bombay. We had all been meeting every day for Bible class, with singing and praise, and so we had gotten to know people. Among them was an elderly Methodist couple. We had gotten to know each other, and this Methodist lady came up and said, "Oh, you're crying." I couldn't say anything, and she put out her arm. "Don't worry dear," she said, and she patted me on my shoulder. "Don't worry, it won't be long. Your term will be over shortly, and then you can go back to your mother."

I wanted to tell her about all I was seeing and feeling, but her vision, her conception of all of that was just absolutely zero. I couldn't say anything for awhile, but then finally I said, "I'm not crying because I'm homesick." And then she walked away. But every once in awhile I think of that, and I still can feel the pathos of that moment.

As Bill said, he was feeling it too, but I don't know where he saw that. He wasn't with me on the deck. But wherever he saw that, it was really something that our very first sight of India impressed us that it was a burden-bearing country.

Bill: Then, of course, we had to go through customs, which to us was a completely new experience. They had little booths. Each customs officer was sitting cross-legged in a little booth, and so each person was assigned to a different customs officer. Joyce was assigned to a different officer than I was. She had a relatively easy time. Mine was not so easy; he made me open up everything that I had, but fortunately I didn't have as much luggage. How many pieces did you have, Joyce?

Joyce: I had eighteen pieces, and Bill only had about three or four.

Bill: I had only three pieces, and Joyce had eighteen. So, if something had to be opened up, it was good that it was mine. But I knew I had a hard time packing my suitcase. There had been four of us that had to literally sit on it in order to get it closed. And I knew that once I opened it, it was going to explode; that's the way it was packed. I told the customs man this. I said, "This one, it will just explode when I open it. You're going to have to hire a number of men to get things back in the way it was."

But I had to open it, and he didn't give me a really hard time, but he made me open everything. I opened that suitcase, and then it did explode. It was sort of a shock to him. He said, "Oh, yes! How can you ever get it all back in?" I said, "I doubt if we can." We didn't, he gave me another box, and so I had an extra box to take from there.

But the humorous thing, where Joyce got a good smile, is that I'm pretty tight with money. At least I was then, in terms of handing out tips and things like that. I'm a bit more generous now than I used to be, but then I was pretty tight. But I got a porter, and Joyce had a different porter, naturally. Then we headed for the train.

Joyce: Going to the train station, that's where I laughed, because of the fellow you paid to help with your luggage.

Bill: Yes, and I said to Joyce, "How much did you pay?" thinking I was going to show her how she should have gotten off paying less. But she paid just a fraction of what I paid! I really got ripped off with the fellow! When we compared, I saw I'd forgotten the notes I had taken on what to pay. I was thinking in terms of our money, not Indian money. At that time it was about eight or nine rupees to one pound sterling. So I paid them eight or nine times more. I paid them in pounds sterling thinking, rather than in rupee thinking. So Joyce paid them correctly.

Joyce: I got off quite lightly that time.

Bill: Getting on the train was quite an experience too, because we'd never been on an Indian train. It was a sleeper, with four berths—two lower berths, two upper berths. We got into the same compartment, Joyce and I, and there was another Indian man. And so, in that small, compact space, there we were for an overnight trip.

Joyce: Three o'clock in the afternoon to eight o'clock in the morning.

Bill: That was sort of traumatic—sleeping in a bedroom with a stranger, in a very small, closed compartment.

Joyce: Even before we got on the train, one of the memories that I have of that train ride was trying to talk to the coolies. We had to try to make them understand what we wanted, or what we thought we wanted, and had to really trust their directions. The Victoria Terminal in Bombay is something else; it's worse than Grand Central in New York. That's because of the crowds, you know, the myriad of people is just awful.

Then when we got on, there was this stranger in our compartment. I had heard so many stories, and I was thinking, "Alone in this sleeping compartment with an Indian man?" He started to talk to us, and he was an Army man, an Army officer. When we got to Poona, which was the first main stop, he offered us coffee, and I said, "No, thank you. No, thank you." I was thinking, "He'll put something in it, make us go to sleep, and then rob us," because we had heard these stories. So there I was, as thirsty as anything, saying "No, thank you, we don't want anything." I wouldn't take anything from him.

He was a gentleman. I mean, he was nice, he talked nicely

and behaved nicely, but there was something in the back of my mind, just because of the things we'd been told in orientation. During the night I hardly slept at all just because I was watching this man. He got off before we did, and that was that. But there were a lot of experiences like this as we first entered into India.

DB: Where were you going to?

Bill: We were going to Secunderabad. From Bombay we were going into Hyderabad state. It's no longer known as Hyderabad state now, because it's been merged into Andrah Pradesh. Going there was an experience also, because Hyderabad state at that time was still under a Moslem ruler, and he had not come into the central union of India. He was holding out for a Moslem state, like Pakistan, right in the heart of India. And the Indian government had surrounded this whole state with their troops, stopped all the flow of food in for months.

That was before we got there. That military barricade had just been lifted a month or two before we arrived when this state had finally said, "Okay, we will come into the Union." But it still had its own customs officers. So at Hyderabad we had to get out of the train, take our bags, and go through customs again. Then we had to pay customs duty, but we had to change our Indian money, which we got at Bombay, into Hyderabadi money to pay the customs and to pay the duty. It was like going into another country, and we were going in and out during our work there. The actual Union came later.

Joyce: Within three years.

Bill: But we were living for a time in a little country within a country. That was another experience showing us the diversity in India. It also helped us to see in a very positive way the almost miraculous steps it took to bring India into unity. It is really remarkable when you think of all of the princely states and kingly states that there were, one of which we entered and lived in for a couple of years before it was brought completely into the Union.

# Chapter 11
# An Unusual Romance

Joyce: After that we were both assigned to the same station at Secunderabad. It was just outside, near the cantonment area. We had been assigned a *pundit*, or a *munchi*, who was a language teacher. We studied an hour or two in the morning with him, then an hour or two in the afternoon, and the rest of the time we were supposed to do our own private study. We were really busy.

About two weeks after we arrived, after breakfast one morning Bill said, "Joyce, would you go for a walk with me after tea?"

I said, "Oh, no, I've got to study."

He said, "Just for a little?"

I said, "No, no, I've got to study." I had a feeling I didn't want to hear what he was going to say.

But after lunch, he asked me again. "Will you go for a walk with me after tea time?"

Again I said, "No," but after teatime, he asked me again. I thought, "Well, it's time to get this fellow off my back," so I said, "Okay, I'll go for a walk with you."

Well, we walked out of the compound and around some of the cantonment area, and then came back into the mission compound area. He started to walk me around a water storage tank there, a cement thing under a mimosa tree, and we were talking and talking.

About halfway around on this walk, I said to him, "Are you proposing?"

And he said, "Well, yes, I guess I am."

I asked him that question because it sounded like he was

asking me to sign a contract. I said, "Look, I don't want to be married." I thought maybe that would stop him in his tracks.

But he just said, "You don't want to be married! What's the matter with you?"

So I briefly told him that I had broken an engagement back in the US, that I had been hurt, and that I had just decided I should serve the Lord with singleness of heart. I told him I didn't want any of this marriage business, with all the involvements and implications. So I said, "Because of that, because I was hurt, this is my decision."

He replied, "I don't plan to hurt you!"

And I thought, "Uh-oh, what kind of a fellow have I got here?"

Then I said, "Bill, we've only just arrived. There are two more girls coming in another couple of weeks, and there are already ten lovely single ladies in this mission. Why don't you give yourself a chance? Get to know them! See who they are!" After all, he was restricting his social contacts, wasn't he? I mean, in two weeks, he hardly knew them. I didn't think he even knew their names. So I said, "Give yourself a chance on this."

He just said, "The Lord didn't tell me to ask them." By this time we had been walking around this tree for a while, and I jokingly said that he just got me so dizzy that I hardly knew what I was saying, going around and around this tree. Anyhow, then I said, "No, Bill, you're a nice fellow, you've got a sense of humor, but I really don't care for you in that way."

Of course these days, you know, if you like somebody, you try to touch their hand, or hold their hand or something like that. He hadn't even attempted that. Well, we had some more discussions there, and finally he said, "Will you pray about it?"

I thought, "Well, I've sounded so weird already, I guess, because of what I said, and I don't want to sound more weird," so I said, "Okay, I will pray about it."

Then he said, "When will you tell me?"

And I thought to myself, "Aha! Got him!" So I told him,

"I'll tell you after a year." You see, my purpose in saying after a year was that it would have given him twelve months to meet these other girls.

Then he asked, "Well, supposing the Lord tells you before a year?" I thought, "Oh my, oh my." And so I just capitulated in a sense. I said, "Well, I guess I would have to tell you when I know." That's what he wanted to hear, anyway, wasn't it?

But, in fact, I did not pray about it. I kept trying to do my language study and trying to forget about what he had asked. I wasn't praying about it, and I didn't want to, although I had said I would. It wasn't long before I could sense during my devotions in the morning that my prayers were hitting the ceiling and coming back down, and I knew exactly why—because I had not yielded in this way.

Finally, after four weeks or so, I decided, "I can't do this. I'm already defeated. I'm only four or five weeks in the field, I'm looking to be a career missionary, and I'm already defeated! Spiritually defeated. This is terrible."

So I said to myself, "OK," and one morning I took my Bible and went up to the rooftop. Those are really safe places over in the East, where they have the rooftops. Bright and early in the morning, I started to pray, and I prayed about everything else I could think of, but again, I wasn't getting anyplace.

So finally I just said, "All right, Lord, now this matter of Bill Scott and his proposal about marriage. You know that I don't love him; he's a nice fellow and all that, but I certainly do not care for him in the way that I think we need to feel for marriage."

Then it just came to me, "Yes, you are to marry him." And I started to argue with the Lord, you know. I argued, "Well, how can I say yes to him when I don't love him?"

And the Lord just said, "It's yes."

So finally, after the battle had gone on and on, raging within, I said, "Well, Lord, if I'm supposed to tell him yes, then I've got to trust You, and I'm asking You to give me the love that is sufficient for marriage by the time we do marry."

Now, I knew that we couldn't marry until we'd been on the mission field a year or had finished our first language exams.

DB: Was that a rule of the mission?

Joyce: Yes, that was the rule of the mission, and a good one. So there was something to comfort me. I went back down, thinking, "Now, how am I going to tell him?"

There was some sort of a weekend conference going on that meant I couldn't see him, so I wrote him a note. I wrote him just plainly, exactly what God had said. I simply wrote, "Bill, you're a nice fellow with good sense of humor, which I enjoy, but I do not love you. However, I believe the Lord is saying yes. Therefore, I will agree to go with you, to date you, whatever, to go together as boyfriend and girlfriend, and trust the Lord to handle the need for that love that is sufficient for marriage. If you don't like this, if you don't want to agree to that at this point, that's fine with me. But this is where I am."

I don't remember whether he answered that by letter or verbally, because after that conference was over, his response to that was, "That's all right with me."

DB: That took a lot of faith on his part.

Joyce: I thought it took more faith on my part!

Bill: I felt that I knew clearly where God wanted me to go. There was one argument I used that Joyce didn't mention. When she said, "Well, you hardly know me," I said, "Look, we've been together for eighteen days on a boat. We've had breakfast together, had mid-morning snacks together, had lunch, afternoon snacks, supper together, and then sitting after supper fellowshipping together in the things of the Lord and so on." I said, "That's for eighteen days. Reckon that time up! If I were dating you an hour or so every night, it would take more than a year of dating. How much more do I need?" I was insistent, but I wanted to get my point across. I said, "How much longer does it take a fellow to know a girl?"

DB: Good point, Joyce!

Bill: I said, "I know you probably better than any boy that

has ever dated you."

**Joyce:** Did you know me better than you knew—what was her name?—Margaret?

**Bill:** In Ireland they don't have six eating times every day as they did on the boat.

**Joyce:** Margaret was a girlfriend in Ireland who refused to consider life on a mission field at all. Anyway, Don, let me give this background because it's really quite amazing.

Reverend Boyer from the York Gospel Center at that time had a summer conference ground called Penn Grove Conference Ground. About two weeks before I left for India, Alfred Ruscoe was there. With Reverend Boyer was Esther Tawney, the lady who happened to be the one who led me to Christ. She was taking care of things at Penn Grove: seeing that the kitchen was functioning properly, that the guests had their beds made, and all the general care of the place. And I was there spending most of the summer to help them any way I could.

When Alfred Ruscoe came to the campground, I remember sitting in the kitchen with Esther and him. Out of the blue he started to share with us this very interesting and very personal story.

## Alfred Ruscoe's Story

Both Alfred and his brother and were so deeply in love with the Lord that they made a pact, a vow, that neither one of them would ever marry and that they would serve the Lord accordingly. So they did live their lives accordingly.

Well, it came time for one of these summer conferences, and they were supposed to be there as speakers. But one week they were just flooded with work in the office, and Alfred made an appeal. He said if there was a typist or stenographer or somebody who could come and stay an extra week, they would give them board and room and everything like that free; they really needed some extra help, and if anybody could come, they'd appreciate that.

There was a young lady who had come with her fiancée

to that conference, and at the end of the week she gave the ring back. They had mutually come to the conclusion that they were not for each other.

So she came into the office to volunteer. When she said, "I have an extra week that I can give," the person in charge of the office said, "Okay, you come in Monday morning."

And so she went in. Later that day, Alfred walked into the office. As he was speaking and taking care of whatever he had to do, he saw this girl. And it just hit him, bang, like that, at which he ran out of that office.

And he prayed, "Lord, what's going on here? Lord, I have promised You. Why have You hit me with this girl, these feelings I suddenly have for this girl? This isn't right. You know that I have committed my life, that my brother and I are Yours totally, nothing else. And we vowed never to marry."

Alfred felt a kind of gentle moving within him that just disturbed him deeply. He found out who the girl was, asked an older, matronly woman what the girl was doing there. "That's the woman who volunteered," said the matron, and she told him as much as she knew.

Then the next day, when his feelings were still there, he called this matronly woman and confided to her what was going on, just the absolute tornado within him, tumultuous feelings and fighting within. The matron asked him, "Well, why don't we bring her in, and talk to her?"

So they asked this girl to come in, and Alfred expressed to her what had happened and what he was feeling. He said to her, "I'm just sharing with you for you to respond in whatever way you want." She said, "Give me twenty-four hours." Well, that was a shocker, that she didn't say, "Hey, go fly a kite."

So they gave her time off. "You go and you take twenty-four hours. If you need more, fine, but don't come into the office; just spend that time with the Lord," which she did. They were to meet the next night.

She came back, and they met the next night. She said, "I believe the Lord is saying yes." Alfred said to her, "I will never ask you to love me, but when you do, I will know it." A few weeks later, they were married.

Alfred concluded his story with this: "I never knew that the Lord had ahead of me the work that He had, but I could not have done it without this girl. I didn't know that at the time. So in faith I had to go and tell her what was going on inside of me, the rushing, all these terrible emotions — terrible in the sense that I was fighting it. And for her to say yes!"

Then he added, "I knew in six months that she loved me, and that this was confirmed by the Lord."

**Joyce:** I had heard that story, you see, just two weeks before I left for India. Then two weeks after I got to India, the same thing happened to me. That was really something! All I could say was, "Lord, thank You for letting me know it does happen!"

**DB:** He prepared you.

**Joyce:** Yes. Where else would you get that kind of preparation, really, except from the Lord? So we had decided then, okay, we would start to date.

Now there was another single man on the station — this is the funny part — who used to ask me to go into the city with him. We would go walking around, shopping and everything, and then he would give me candy. At times I would offer Bill some of the candy. This was before, wasn't it?

**Bill:** This was before.

**Joyce:** Yes, during that period of time when I wasn't answering Bill. Bill asked, "Hey, where are you getting all this candy?" And I said, "Oh, Leonard's giving it to me," to which Bill said, "Here this fellow is, and day after day we're on our knees together in our room…"

**Bill:** He was my roommate; we were in the same room.

**Joyce:** Yes, they were roommates. Leonard was saying,

"Pray with me, Bill, I don't have money, I haven't got any money."

Bill: He was praying every day that he needed money, and I was taking it out of my pocket, you know, "Here, brother, here's a couple of rupees, here's ten rupees for your needs, for your toothpaste or whatever." And then I find out that he's spending it on chocolate for you!

Needless to say, that night I spoke to Leonard. "No more praying like that. You're not getting any more money from me!"

Joyce: So, anyhow, after I wrote to Bill and told him how I responded to him, this other fellow wrote me a note and proposed in a note to me. So I went to Bill and showed him the letter, and he read it. Here was Leonard proposing to me. Bill just said, "Well, I'll talk with him."

So for the second time he had to go and tell Leonard "hands off," that I wasn't available. Bill told him that we had decided after prayer that we were going together, seeing what God would do for us. Way off there in the middle of India, Bill was having competition, which usually doesn't happen. There are many more women missionaries than there are bachelors. Anyway, soon after that, I was transferred out to where all those lovely missionary girls were, in Bhongir, about thirty miles away.

DB: Was the language study difficult for you? Americans often have more trouble with language study than Europeans, since they all have more contact with people who speak other languages.

Joyce: It was not too bad. But some funny things always happen in connection with language study, some funny mistakes. We had to read a portion of Scripture, and we had to translate it into Telugu and give it back. It was during our second year, and we were studying Acts. I was supposed to give back to the teacher the story about the man with the virgin daughters who went around prophesying. I was diligently, and so sincerely, talking about this and telling the story, and I said that the virgins were going around giving birth to children!

Bill: The thing is, there are two very similar words.

Joyce: There are two words—one is *pravasinsu*, and the other is *prasavinsu*. I got them mixed up, and I was saying, instead of that they were going around prophesying,…

Bill: *Pravasinsu* is prophesying.…

Joyce: … Instead I said they were going around *prasavinsuing*, giving birth—virgins giving birth to children! The teacher looked at me. He said, "Do you want to repeat that again?" I said, "Sure." I repeated the same thing again. He asked me five times to repeat that, and suddenly it came to me that I was using the wrong word, and it's just transposing two consonants. There were times like that with the language.

One of my first modes of witnessing, when we would go out with Mr. Steenstra, who was the senior missionary on our station, was playing my harmonica. Bill was not there at the time; he was some other place. We would go out to the village, and sometimes we would stay overnight.

Bill: A very, very godly man.

DB: Dutch?

Bill: Yes. Well, he was American of Dutch descent, and he was a godly man.

Joyce: One thing I had brought with me in all that luggage was a phonograph that you could also use for a P.A. system. And until I learned the language, all I could do was to play the harmonica. So the villagers would see this white woman in the middle of the village, blowing this mysterious thing, and it really brought out a crowd. So we didn't have a problem drawing an audience to our village gospel meetings. That was my little contribution for the first year or so, helping to draw people to hear the Gospel.

DB: And all this time Bill was thirty-six miles away?

Bill: I used to go there on weekends, or Joyce would come in.

Joyce: They had planned to put a language school in the headquarters, and then found that it was not possible at that time because of problems with logistics and accommodations. So I went to Bhongir, and Bill stayed on at the headquarters. It was January 8th, after our successfully passing the first language exams, that we were married.

Bill: But there was one more hitch before that happened. The rule was that you had to pass your language exam first, and you did your written exam a week before you did your oral exam. You could not do the oral unless you passed the written.

Both of us did our written exams, and we both passed, so we both appeared with all the other missionaries for the oral. And the oral exam was in three parts. First they tested your skills in reading the Bible and poetry in Telugu. Then you had a session where they gave you a Bible passage or verse and you gave an exposition on it, so they tested your skills of giving an exposition on a passage. The third part was general conversation, which always led into a question about the ministry you're going into.

We all knew the question: "What are you going to do after this exam?" And then your answer had to be, "I'm going to go into nursing," and they will channel the conversation into nursing. Or you would say, "I'm going to go into church planting," or "I'm going into evangelism," or "I'm going into teaching," whatever. Then they would channel the conversations into your field.

So we both did our first two sessions, and for the third session, going in alphabetical order, S came before Y. So I went in, and the panel of examiners asked, "Bill, what are you going to do after this exam?"

I had an answer prepared for them. I said, "That's up to you."

That shocked them. They said, "What do you mean, that's up to us?"

I said, "Well, if you pass me, I'm going to get married. If I don't pass, I'm not going to get married. It's up to you!"

And they said, "That's not the answer we wanted!"

I said, "I know, but you asked me what I'm going to do; well, that's the immediate thing that I'm going to do."

So the whole conversation was finished by then. It was only a five- or ten-minute conversation by the time we got through the joke, and we did it in Telugu. And they said, "Okay, it's finished."

The panel is made up of missionaries and Indians, and as I was walking out, the chairman said, "Bill, you can get married."

Then I said, "Well, there's a girl following me, she has to pass, too!"

He said, "You really drive a hard bargain!"

I said, "If she doesn't pass, I won't be able to get married." Well, she did pass.

*Joyce:* They didn't know who it was.

*Bill:* I didn't tell them who the girl was. They knew, I think, but I didn't tell them. There were several girls following me, as well as several fellows. But I thought, I'm going to go in there and tell them, and throw them off, and just get them.

And so we got married.

# The Scott Family Album

## York Meets Belfast in London

What we looked like when we first met in London on October 11, 1950.

**Joyce M. Yost**

**William Scott**

## Voyages

We sailed on this from Tilbury, England, to Bombay, India.

Arrival date: October 28, 1950

### Our Wedding Day
January 8, 1952, in Bhongir, India

# The Scott Family Album

## Family Portraits

**May 1974 — The Scotts**

**1987 — Shanti, Jyothi John, Bill, Joyce, Terry, Beth**

# The Scott Family Album

## Recent Portraits

**Rev. Dr. Joyce M. Scott**

**Rev. Dr. William Scott**

**Terry Lee Scott**
Population Control & Entrepreneur

**Elizabeth Hartzell**
Psychotherapy Technician

**Shanti Joy Scott**
R.N.

**Jyothi John Scott**
C.T. and MRI Technician

# Chapter 12

# First Assignment

**D**B: With language school and the wedding behind them, Bill and Joyce were given their first assignment: a school in the village of Peddapalli. You have already read about the house they lived in and the snakes they met. You have read about Bill's encounter with the booksellers in the bazaar, and his vision for getting the Word of God into the hands of the Indian people. The school itself is another interesting story, and I asked Joyce to tell it.

Joyce: I was the only missionary who had a four-year degree with teacher training, so they asked me to be the principal of the school in Peddapalli. Because of his training as an accountant, Bill was made the business manager.

When we got there, we found the school rather disorganized. There were about thirty kids, but nobody knew what grade they were in. At first, the challenge was just to set things straight, to try to make a proper school out of it. But the longer we were there, the more I felt the burden for it to become a school that would truly meet the needs of the children.

It did not have government recognition, what might be called accreditation here, so the children who were attending it could not go on to any more schooling. They would finish five or six years, go home, and pick herbs out of the ground. That would be about it; they would have nothing they could do. So we started what was called "Basic Education."

Basic Education was a term made popular by Mahatma Gandhi in his days of power and influence in India. By that he meant teaching basic cottage crafts to children in school so that they could go back home and earn a living, having learned a productive skill.

I was all for this, but they did not have any syllabus. I had one teacher who was more trained than others. His name was Paranjyothi, which means "heavenly light." He and I worked together writing a syllabus for various skills. We taught tailoring, poultry raising, carpentry, keeping home kitchen gardens from which they could sell the produce, taping, that is making tape for beds, and…

Bill: Peanut butter!

Joyce: Yes, we experimented with making peanut butter. We taught any kind of productive craft we could think of for those who could not go on to more schooling. Even the government district officer, they call him the District Educational Officer, came to me and asked me whether I would give him that syllabus so that he could give it to his government schools.

Bill Teate: What's really amazing, Don, is how you'll see when we hear about the huge literacy programs they developed, that all this turned out to be beautifully useful preparation! I'm sure they didn't think of it that way at the time, but that's how God works.

Joyce: The Lord was in this all the way, and as Bill Teate has just said, I never thought of it like that, actually. But we kept going. We added qualified teachers, we added rooms, we added students, we got a little science equipment, we set up a little laboratory—we just did all the things we were supposed to do.

We worked and sweated for that government recognition. The District Educational Officer, with whom I was dealing, would come and say, "All right, Mrs. Scott, you still have to do this, this, and this." We would have to do those things to be approved by him. And we kept making progress, doing what he said.

But our concern was not just for those who went on to more schooling. We also worked on teaching those major crafts, things they could do as cottage industries to improve their lives.

Bill: And the school kept growing.

Joyce: The school kept growing. After four years it was really doing well. But then, that year in the fall we were called by the Field Council of India Mission. We were told that we could not do anything further. They told us, "You may not make any further approach to the government officers to get this school recognized." They thought the government would try to control it, take over the policies, so that we couldn't teach anything about Jesus.

If you take government money, then, yes, they can come in and say, "You do this, this, and this." But we were not after government money. We just wanted official recognition. So when the mission said, "You can't ask for it anymore," I went to the staff, and I said, "Okay. These people are saying we cannot make any further approach to the DEO. Do you still want recognition?"

"Yes, yes, we want recognition."

"Then it's prayer." Then all of us just got on our knees and prayed. At Christmas time, word of the government recognition came, during the Christmas vacation, without our having had any further contact with the government. It just came, an answer to our prayers. In the mail came the final papers from the government: "Your school has been recognized." Also the very day we were to leave for our first furlough, we got the certified, sealed, registered mail packet of official government exams. The beautiful part of it is that every one of our students passed that first government exam with flying colors. We had 100% pass.

Bill: That is really significant in India, because the usual percentage of passing in government schools in India is only, I don't know, about…

Joyce: …About thirty or forty percent.

Bill: So when you have a school with 100% pass, that makes it immediately a prestigious school. And, of course, as things went on after they received recognition, the enrollments really grew.

*Joyce:* Once the school was recognized up to seventh grade, every year we were able to add one more year: eighth, ninth, tenth, like that. So it got to be a fully recognized Telugu-medium school, a school where subjects are taught in the Telugu language.

And here is an added blessing. When we came back from that first furlough, the first man to whom I had ever given employment at that school was a warden and a teacher. He was a young fellow by the name of David, the first Indian I employed. He had only had an eighth grade education, but he also had teacher training. He became the warden. He loved Jesus like anything, and so when he was there, he began to study privately. He finished his high school, continued to study privately, finished his bachelor's degree, continued to study, and finished his master's.

Now, when I turned the school over, he took over and became principal. And this man also started an English-medium school, with subjects taught in the English language. That has more educational prestige. That school had about 300 or 400 students in it, but now it has gone on to become a junior college, and there are about 1,300 students who attend.

*DB:* How many years were you in the school?

*Joyce:* Until 1961, about nine years.

*Bill:* An interesting footnote is that the first qualified teacher to ever be at that school was Joyce. Up until then they'd never had a qualified teacher. Not one was qualified. And the first national qualified teachers that were brought to that school were brought by Joyce. This, for some reason, made our older missionaries nervous. I don't know why. But that's why the school got to where it is, and that's why we find that the fathers of a number of the leaders in the churches today went through this struggle with us, through the same agony that Joyce and I went through.

Several times in those years we were threatened by the mission and told we would be sent home if we didn't start toeing the line. But Joyce was adamant, and she kept trying to improve the school. When they said, "No more," we did no more. We obeyed. But God intervened, and we got the recognition for the school, and that is a big part of why we have such an opening in India today. To me, it's really miraculous that this little village school has been so significant in the last 25 years, the years following the first 25 when we were in that village. It has been so significant that all I can say is, it was God. God put us there.

As we look back over that era of our time spent in the villages, one of the highlights was the time we spent at that school. Then it seemed more like an experience in the far side of a desert. But today we are finding leaders in India, not just in the church but also in professions, in business,…

Joyce: And government…

Bill: …and in government, who were our students at that school. We have India open to us partly because of the advancement those village kids were able to make from that school. They tell us that they're indebted to us. They say publicly: "We would not be where we are if it had not been for the Scotts and the education they gave us so that we could get on." Even here in America, I was introduced at a conference, and when the man said my name, an Indian who was there at the back got up and said, "Dr. Scott, my teacher!" Publicly! Here! He said, "That's the man of God who brought me to where I am today. I thank God for him and for the school at Peddapalli." So in retrospect, that is one of the highlights.

Joyce: And that could not have happened if we had not struggled and done all we had to do to get the school recognized…

Bill: Agonized.

Joyce: It really was agonizing. Without official recognition for the school, students would have gone back to the village, and that would have been it.

Bill: And that's only part of the work and the ministry of those years.

*Chapter 13*

# Branches, Partners, and Growth

**D**B: All during the years of building the school at Peddapalli, the Scotts never lost sight of their primary vision: getting the Word of God into the hands of the Indian people. Their "free time" was spent in doing, thinking, planning, and building partner relationships, all focused on sowing the seed. Their official connections changed from time to time as they felt God directing their work, but the energy and the focus never changed. And, as always, things that did not seem central to the plan when they happened often turned out later to be wonderfully helpful. For instance, five years before they left the school in Peddapalli, …

*Joyce:* When we went home on our first furlough, the director of the labs in Abington Hospital gave me the opportunity to study medical technology during that year. So when we got back this time, I was able to add some laboratory facilities to the "back door dispensary" out of our house in the village. Then government doctors often referred patients to me for lab work. I was also able to work in a Church of South India mission hospital in Karimnagar. I used to go over once in a while by bus or by car to spend a day or two there helping them in the lab.

That also turned out to be preparation for what happened later, for when we left the India Mission, we were accepted by the Church of South India and stationed at that hospital.

*Bill:* That happened in 1961.

*Joyce:* Bill was business manager for the hospital, and I

was supervisor of the laboratory.

Bill found that across the street from the hospital was a vacant room, a little room that could be rented. In the meantime, Benjamin Krupanidhi left Peddapalli, where his wife was a teacher, and came over to join us. He was feeling led to follow Bill's challenge and burden to become a *colporteur*, someone who distributes Bibles and Christian literature. Bill rented that room. We outfitted it as a reading room and that's what it became for the area there. We got a daily newspaper along with Bibles and Christian books. Benjamin Krupanidhi ran that, but he would also go out to the various villages and distribute Gospels.

And here's a story I've never forgotten. He had the Gospels, and he was going through the houses in a particular village. He went to one house, and the lady saw what he had, and he told her what it was. He said, "A way to happiness, a way to new life."

She said, "I don't have any money. How much is it?"

It was just going to be ten pice, which is what, Bill? A cent or something?

Bill: No, just a fraction of a cent.

Joyce: She said, "No, I don't even have that." Then she said, "Wait a minute. Will you just wait for a minute?"

He said, "Yes, I'll wait."

So she called her son, she gave him two eggs that she had just bought that morning for her family. She sent him back to the bazaar to sell the eggs back to the man and bring the ten pice so that she could buy that Gospel. You know, I've never forgotten that, and I admire that woman, who was full of such longing to hear these words of life.

Bill: Joyce has brought us up to the time when God—and it's in retrospect that we're saying this—but this is about the time when God began to open up the nation of India. I have a theory that it took India almost two decades to realize that it was a free country. It was free, but the people didn't know. They didn't know that they were free to do what they wanted.

There was a deep fear, a psychosis from those years, that stopped them taking the Word of God. Now they were getting over that. That's my theory.

If anyone asks me to prove it, I have no hard evidence, except that something happened. Things changed. People were opening up. They were coming to a Christian book room, which they wouldn't have done before. Our book room was busy. People were coming and buying from the shelves the Christian books and Bibles that were there.

DB: How did Benjamin Krupanidhi come to know of you or Joyce so that he would respond to his desire to serve in this way?

Joyce: The school in Peddapalli run by the India Mission had invited us to lead a retreat for the faculty. I couldn't go, but Bill went and met him that weekend.

DB: His wife was a teacher in the school?

Joyce: Yes, Sarah was his wife, teaching at the Peddapalli school where we had been. And they had been urging us, "Please come back to Peddapalli!" We felt we were where we were supposed to be, so we didn't go. But when they asked Bill to go speak that weekend he did. He shared with them the burden we felt for what we were doing. Krupanidhi came to him after the services and said, "I have that burden too; I share that burden. May I come?" And Bill said, "Okay, you can come."

At the time his wife was making several hundred rupees a month, and he was just an itinerant evangelist. When he came, he accepted a salary of 62 rupees a month. It was about 4.5 rupees to the dollar, at that time.

Bill: He came for less than $15 a month.

Joyce: I was amazed. He simply said, "That's all right. Whatever God gives me, that's it." He just took that burden on, just took that responsibility and that challenge, and he's been with us ever since. He's still working with us. He, if anybody, has seen the growth of the literature work, because we called this Glad Tidings Distributors. That was the first name of our literature work, and it started with that reading room.

DB: What is Krupanidhi's position with you now?

Bill: Before I tell you, let me explain that small amount of money we offered. The policy that I have in India, and always have had, is that if anyone comes and says he has a calling from God, I respect that, but I will then not induce them by money. I say, "If you have a calling of God, you're welcome to come and work. But you look to God and not to me." That is why I offered such a low amount.

Joyce: Well, we didn't have money either.

Bill: That's true. We didn't have money to give more, and that's why I said, "I'm trusting God, and I will trust God for this with you," and he was willing to do that.

Krupanidhi came as a salesman, and I was a salesman, too, so we both were on the same level. I wasn't a boss. It wasn't a boss to worker relation. We both were servants of God—that's what we were called in India—and I was doing the same work that he was doing. When I came out of my office in the hospital, I was out in the villages, and he was out in the villages.

In effect, he became a disciple, and he treated me as the Indians treat a teacher—a guru, as they call them. That was the relationship, although I wasn't an old guru. We were close to the same age.

So he has gone through what we have gone through. And, of course, he knew our lifestyle; he knew that we were renting the same kind of a bungalow, the same kind of house in which he was living. He knew that. And he didn't know any other missionaries that were doing that, because there were none around that area.

Joyce: They used to live in big compounds, you know, with the big walls around them, six- or seven-foot high walls. They lived in great big huge stone houses. They called them bungalows, but they were big rambling places. We just had a little place, the same kind of place the Indians were living in.

Bill: It wasn't the fault of the missionaries, really; it was just that the British had ruled India, so they built fortresses for missionaries, their missionaries. They literally isolated their preachers. That was the custom at that time, and many missionaries just came in and occupied those buildings, those big houses and those big mansions. It's not that they built them, but the mansions were there, so they occupied them. We, by choice, did not live like that, and Krupanidhi knew this.

He has worked and lived with us right through, and he's still with us. Now he's director of South India Bible Literature. He's a Regional Director, he's on our management committee, and he is a board advisor. He is a senior member of the staff today. But he never has forgotten our roots, and I haven't either.

We often reflect on where we came from and what God has done with the weak things of the world to confound the mighty, as He promised in 1 Corinthians 1:27. Krupanidhi knows that; he knows how weak we were, and how God has taken our weakness to confound the mighty. So it's really a beautiful story.

It seems as though there was some great change every ten or twelve years. India was very closed to the Gospel up to 1961, and at that time it was just beginning to open. Then ten years later there was another big change. In 1971 the floodgates began to open. And just at that time the World Home Bible League came to India, saw the work that we were doing. John DeVries had just come on the staff of World Home Bible League. He and Bill Ackerman, the director of World Home Bible League, came to India, met me, and saw the work of Glad Tidings Distributors, and everything else that was going on.

By that time it had developed into multiple bookstores, and we had several dozen *colporteurs*, like Benjamin Krupanidhi, working under him. What's more, they were all basically self-supporting. They were not paid a salary; they got ten percent of what they sold, so that it operated on a self-supporting basis. It had to.

We did not set up a mission organization, with a budget, to do a ministry. We were doing a ministry, and it developed into a mission organization. It was just backwards from how mission work is often done.

At that time we had no organization employing people; we just had people doing ministry. This was bringing us to the necessity of organizing, and that's when the World Home Bible League asked me to become their director for India. I agreed. Then they said, "But you're going to need an office."

DB: Who was it that said you needed an office?

Bill: Bill Ackerman said that, and I had to agree with him that it was necessary. It did not come from me, but I did feel that God was moving us to get that administrative structure to support the ministry.

Then I had a decision to make about finances. They offered to pay for the office, which I refused, because I did not want a paid administrative structure controlling a ministry. It was a decision I have never regretted. So I rejected a policy of a structure coming in to develop a ministry. Instead, I maintained what God gave me, which was my calling under God, a ministry that necessitates an administrative structure. I made a decision that the administrative costs would be paid from the ministry work, and that all outside money would go directly to ministry. That is how we still operate in IBL, India Bible Literature.

DB: Could you expand on that a bit? It doesn't sound like the usual way of doing things, and it needs to be understood.

Bill: Bill Ackerman asked us to open an office. I said, "Yes, we need a secretary, somebody to be writing letters and keeping records, and a place for this work." They said, "We will set it up and pay those costs." I said, "No, I will not take that. Whatever money you would have paid for that, give it for Bibles." So they did; they gave us more money for Bibles. We distributed more Bibles, and so the ministry grew. Then out of the funds generated from the ministry, from distributing Bibles, we paid for the office.

The ministry supported the administration, which is still the principle that we're following today. Of course, we were talking about supporting just one office clerk at that time. Now it's larger.

DB: So then no money given from America today goes to pay any administrative costs in India; is that right?

Bill: That's right. That's what I said. I made that decision then as a young missionary, and I don't regret it. I'm glad, and I believe that was under God. I mean, I was making the decision, but I believe that's what God was leading us to do.

At that time, I bought a little wooden table, a wooden chair, one person sitting on it, so we're talking of a hundred or two rupees a month for the whole administrative structure. If you want to jump ahead forty years, to what we're doing now, that same administrative office now costs about eighty million rupees per year. That's what the administrative structure of IBL is today. So what God has done is just nothing short of a miracle.

DB: That's about two million dollars. And it's all supported from the work in India?

Bill: That's right. No outside money goes toward the administration; all of it goes to ministry.

DB: Nobody's salary is being paid from America?

Bill: Nobody's. Every salary in India is paid from India. In that connection it is important to say that we were beginning to develop a partnership base in India that was getting broader and broader, penetrating more and more into the nation.

Then we started to develop other programs that supported and complemented the basic vision of getting the Word of God to the people of India. For example, we started having some special events for children; we started having some conferences for evangelists and pastors to challenge them and their churches to get involved in getting the Word of God out.

This kind of activity brought us into partnership in ministry with the Church of South India, the Church of North India, the Lutheran Church of India, the Presbyterian Church of India, the Independent Pentecostal churches, the Brethren Assembly—all of these now were becoming partners with India

Bible Literature.

In America at that time we were working with the American Baptists. They were paying our salary.

Joyce: Well, we were American Baptists.

Bill: We were American Baptist missionaries, so we did what the American Baptists wanted us to do. I was administrator of a hospital and taught in the seminary. Joyce was in charge of the clinical laboratory and literacy work under the American Baptists.

So they gave us work to do. But we also asked them, "Would we be free to develop India Bible Literature?"

They responded, "Yes, you would be free to do that."

So we were building India Bible Literature in addition to what the American Baptists assigned us to do.

Then when the World Home Bible League came to us, we arranged for them to have a written understanding with the American Baptists. They had a work of distributing Scriptures, and they plugged that into the work that we were doing. We said yes, that fits into what God has called us to do. We will do that for you.

DB: The goal of the World Home Bible League was a Bible for every home?

Bill: Yes. They were distributing two to three thousand a year when I took over as director. I know that because I was the only distributor. Then the number of Bibles distributed grew very significantly from that level because they plugged into an existing organization. By that time we had dozens of evangelists directly under us, and hundreds partnering with us. If they had tried to set up from scratch, they could not have done it. But they worked through us. They were wise, and I was happy. That was one partnership.

Then other partnerships started to come to IBL. And how this happened was just word of mouth. For example, World MAP, World Missionary Assistance Plan, wanted to open up in India. They did research in India to try to find some Indians or an organization that could do their work, instead of setting up their own. Their man was in India, and he had been there for about two months, but he had given up. They couldn't find anything. Then somebody told him, "Why don't you talk to…?"

Joyce: He went home; he went home to Ralph Mahoney and told Ralph. Ralph said, "I have just been given the name of Bill Scott in Madras. Go back and find him."

Bill: So this man came back to me, told me the story that I've just told you now, that's how I knew. He said, "Bill, we've heard about you," and he saw what we had, and he got excited. He said, and I'm trying to quote him accurately, "This is God's answer to prayer. I've been agonizing before God to get what I'm seeing today. You have it." And he added, "Will you take on our project?"

Then he told me what it was. It was to get a magazine into the hands of church leaders that would bring spiritual renewal and quickening. They had very small circulation at that time. I don't have the figure in my head, but it was small. And he said, "Would you take that over? Could you print the magazine?"

By this time we were beginning to get experience in printing, warehousing, and distribution. It was still small compared to where we are now, but it was big then. He again asked, "Could you?" And I said, "Yes, we can do it."

That necessitated more workers then. I explained to him my principle, that I did not want him to pay any worker in India, which excited him. He asked, "Not pay any workers?" My answer was no.

But he said, "You're going to need, I mean, we're talking of enlarging your staff by perhaps six people, which is significant. How will you pay them?"

I said, "You give me the money to produce the materials. We'll get the work done, and from that we will pay."

He said, "That's terrific. No one told me that."

I'm telling you what he was telling me. I said, "That's the way we work." So that was another partner coming in.

Now I'm skipping over years, but I'm telling you how partners develop. This is the story of another partner. I went over to Ireland. My nephew there said, "Uncle Billy, I want to bring you to meet someone who wants to get to know you, and to another man who already knows you."

So we went to what is called Revival Movement in Ireland. It's a place that produces booklets and Gospels for distribution to the world. Their ministry is to produce these and get them out to the nations of the world. They had nothing going in India except a few requests here and there. They were sending boxes here and there in India, but it was a small work.

My nephew introduced me to the young fellow who was now in charge, but the founder of that mission already knew me. He was my age, my generation. He knew me better than I knew him. On reflection, as he shared where we met, I began to realize how he had gotten to know me.

We talked and they wanted to know what we were doing in India. I told him and shared something of the vision, and his eyes lit up. He said, "Is this what you're up to?" And he said, "Well, we want to open in India. Do you think you could handle anything like that?"

When I said, "I think so," he asked, "Could you give a figure off the top of your head of what you think you could do in a year?" So I gave my estimate of we could do in a year.

DB: He was talking about Scriptures?

Bill: Scriptures. The number I gave him was so big, he said, "I've never heard of a figure like that in my life!"

I said, "You asked me what we could do in a year."

He said, "I like it. You have challenged us more than anybody in the world." It was just a simple little conversation. I honestly did not know I was challenging him. I was just sharing with him. I was a little bit more enthusiastic in those days than I am today, but I was just sharing with him, you know, what God was doing, and what I felt we could do with God's strength.

DB: If you were more enthusiastic then than now, I'm not sure I could have survived meeting you then!

Bill: Anyway, that started another partnership. It was very

small at that time. We undertook to distribute the maximum that he could give, which was about three or four pallets, less than half of a shipping freight container load a year. That was the maximum they could do then.

DB: So they printed books in Ireland?

Bill: They had their own press there with volunteers. They printed books…

Joyce: And tracts.

Bill: Books, booklets, tracts. They sent them to India, and we sent them to their customers, which were very few in India. But we opened up the market in India so that today, from that organization, I get at least one container a month, and they are talking of increasing that. A container a month is a lot of books and booklets and tracts, and they have already put in two brand new large web offset presses, just for India. That was another partnership.

I asked him recently, "How many containers a year do you ship?" About twenty was his answer.

I said, "Twenty? Worldwide?"

And he said, "Yes."

"And we get twelve!" I said.

He laughed. "Bill, you are our major partner."

Today, for that organization, India is about 85-90% of their ministry. And it's a beautiful partnership, because not only do they donate all the books and booklets to us, but they're also printing some of our books for us, which saves us millions of dollars. We're talking big money that they put into the ministry. Not only that, but they pay us for packing and shipping to their customers. We never asked them to do that, but voluntarily they pay IBL for packing and shipping. We would happily do it free, but they say, "No, no. We will pay you; you are a faith mission, and we are a faith mission."

I could go on and on about our many partnerships. This is the way partnerships have opened and developed overseas. And these partnerships have known what the ministry of IBL is, and then plugged into the resources that IBL has. We will not take any partnership that does not complement the vision that God has given us.

We have refused a number of very fine partnerships. Some excellent worldwide orphanage organizations have asked us to open orphanages, but I said, "That's not our calling in God," even though they've offered to fund it all.

We've been offered printing presses. I said, "We're not called to be printers, we're called to get the Word of God printed, but we can do it better in commercial presses with less headache and more economically. Now we could have a printing press of our own. I've refused several large printing presses that would have brought in a hundred or two workers and would have given us a large plant.

So we have refused a number of good ministries because, as I have frequently said, that it can be a temptation from Satan, not just to do wrong things, but to do good things that are out of the will of God for you. They're within the will of God, but for other people. In other words, it can be wrong to take somebody else's ministry and do that when that's not what God wants you to do.

Bill Teate: Stay focused on God's calling for you.

Bill: By God's grace, He has enabled us to keep focused on the vision. We're not focused in the sense that we've got tunnel vision, being so narrow that we couldn't see complementary things, such as literacy and other things that would complement that vision. But we're focused in that we won't deviate out of that broad area of our calling.

That's why I say the vision is a progressive one: we're progressively moving with God. Quite honestly, I don't know in the next decade what God will bring IBL, progressively. All I know is that it's not a static vision; there will be progression.

Bill Teate: I know one other principle that you've stood on, Bill. It's the principle that money must not control ministry. For example, if someone from America said to you, "We'll give you money but you must do the things we want done."

Bill: That's true. That is a principle that we have stood on.

You do not determine your calling — at least we do not determine our calling in God — by the amount of money that is available for any specific thing.

For example, the partnerships that I said we refused. There was an orphanage that had a budget of several million dollars. That's a nice amount of money to be handling for a year. It was coming in through radio programs. They were not on television in those days. It was radio, and they were getting significant funding. That was a nice amount of money, but I said no to that, not because that ministry is wrong, but because that ministry was not the ministry that God wanted us to do.

Actually, I do not know where I got all that I am. I think I got it from reading. I mean, God implanted all of these ideas in my spirit from books. I read Mueller and Taylor and Hyde, and I suddenly see I'm doing what they did. I didn't set out to copy them, but I think some of the principles that God worked in their lives, He also worked in my life. And this is where I am.

My struggle is not for money. I very seldom ask God for money, even in my private prayers. I don't publicly, but even in private I very seldom ask God for money. So I don't agonize for money. Money, by the grace of God, has not had an appeal to me.

People have come and offered substantial amounts through a certain ministry, which I didn't feel was of God for us, so I said no to them. They were sort of shocked. "But we're giving you the money!"

"But that's not what I'm here for. I'm here to do the work of God. Somebody else is going to do what you want to fund, but you find that somebody else. It's not me."

I agonize with God to know, "Am I doing what You want me to do, in the way in which You want me to do it?" Two things — one, to do the right thing; and second, not only to do the right thing, but to do the right thing in the right way. If I get those two things straight, I'm at peace. I don't worry about the third. That's God's problem, actually. He has to supply, and I don't.

# Chapter 14

# Demons, Mantras, and the Spirit of God

**D**B: I want to ask you, Bill, if I may, a question that comes out of my father's experience. He grew up in California, and as a young man went to the Bible Institute of Los Angeles, which at that time was headed by Dr. C. I. Scofield, editor of the Scofield Bible. R. A. Torrey was there teaching, and many other well-known ministers. He later studied under Warfield and Machen at Princeton. Warfield taught that there was no operation of the Spirit in the church today as there was in Bible times, that all that was temporary while the Scripture was being written. Scofield had been very much against the charismatic Azusa Street revival, which was just a few blocks away from the Bible Institute of Los Angeles. So my Dad had been taught that such things were not an authentic part of Christian life today. Along with that, he had serious reservations about stories of demon possession in modern times, in what was called "the church age."

But then in 1934, he went around the world. He had been given a foundation grant to visit the mission stations of the Presbyterian Church. He spent sixteen months on the trip and visited most of the missions of other denominations in the nations on his itinerary, too. When he got to India, he said he was shocked by what he saw and what he heard from the missionaries, by the sense that the demonic presence was very real and very powerful.

Bill: Right. It is.

DB: Tell me about that, as you experienced it when you

got to India. Had you already believed and expected to see that, or was it a surprise to you, and how did you feel it when you got there?

Bill: Well, I came out of the Anglican Church, which was the particular church I went to, and it was very liberal, so I didn't get much Bible teaching as a youngster in that setting. I got my Bible memorization in school as I mentioned, and then I went to the Baptist Church, the Irish Baptist Church, which is very conservative, but which is also against belief in the gifts of the Spirit in our time.

The explanation you cited is the stand they take, that the day, the age of the miraculous is gone, and that was only for that small period of time during the lifetime of the apostles. So I came out of that same kind of teaching as your father did.

But in spite of coming out of that, I did not really go completely along with them. I acknowledged within myself that the supernatural was real, the supernatural power in the now, both of good and evil. I didn't go to India expecting to see anything. I didn't go with any kind of expectations. But I did not go with any preconceived ideas that I was not going to be confronted with demonic powers that would be real.

My first exposure — well, actually I'm not sure I remember my first exposure — let me say that my early exposures to the demonic did impress me, because India is indeed a country where the power of the demonic can be felt, as your father observed, and as the missionaries he talked with had observed.

It's not something that you can understand or grasp with your intellect alone. It's really a power that is felt and known. You know that it is a power there. My early exposures to it were real, at some of the large Hindu festivals where people give themselves over to demonic possession, where there is the worship of Satan and the releasing of the power of Satan in the lives of the worshippers.

I had a feeling of shock, but not shock to the extent that it was something totally new. It was something that I intellectually knew was possible because of the accounts of demons in the Gospels, unclean spirits. So it wasn't the kind of shock where my whole theological stand was challenged. It was just a shock to see it in its rawness, in its openness, in the way that it could be felt.

My early exposures were at some of the Jatras, the festivals, where we went when we were studying language. I had seen them in Bhongir, where I had been visiting Joyce. She had been in Bhongir except for the few weeks she was in Trimulgherry. I came there after we were married, and we went to one of these Jatras to give out Gospels. We stayed overnight, slept in the car, or just slept out on the ground, like everybody else does. The festivities go on for twenty-four hours a day without stopping.

At that time I came face to face with demon possession, where I saw people demonically possessed, out of their senses, and where they were demonstrating a power, a physical power that was superhuman. They were also demonstrating a power to suffer pain that was superhuman. They cut and lacerated themselves, doing it in ways that, in the natural, should have been impossible. They should have been screaming. It's also something that you wouldn't naturally do if you were in your right mind. I don't mean just little pinpricks; I mean lacerations. I came across that in this festival.

By that time perhaps, I wasn't in as much shock as in the initial encounters, but I felt a very deep sorrow, a sorrow to tears. I stood there and cried out, "Oh, God, I'm a youngster," — and I was; we were just started in our mission career — "God, I'm a youngster, being confronted now with a power that is real, that is definite, that is strong. I need Your power in a way that will be as evident as this in order for me to stand, in order for me to have any kind of ministry in the nation of India."

At that time I did not have the power of God in me. I was still the traditional Baptist missionary, but I was committed to God unconditionally, and that never wavered. But I cried out to God, "I have to have Your power in my life, which I know is greater than any of the powers that I'm seeing around me."

So while it was awesome to see this, I never lost sight of the awesomeness and the greatness of the God that we serve. That, I believe, is what sustained me in India. Certainly no one with eyes to see could visit a nation like India and come away and say, "I do not believe in demons." You would have to be totally blinded to be able to go there and still say, "I do not believe in demons." Either that or totally protected from the real India by always staying in the environment of a five-star hotel.

You might also go in a totally protected seminary setting, where you're in a seminary compound and never go out of the compound to see this. That happens. And such people come back and say, "Well, I saw nothing that would change my mind on the demonic."

But certainly if you move in the streets of India, if you move around where the people are, and particularly if you get into some of the festivals, which are very, very evil, dramatic in their evil, then you would be convinced.

DB: Are they worshipping Kali or Shiva?

Bill: Kali is one of the bad ones, and you find that cult in Calcutta. And to this day, if I get caught up in the Kali festivals in Calcutta—I don't go to attend any! I never would!—but if I'm walking the street and there happen to be two or three Kali processions that come, then naturally I'm absorbed into the crowds of people who are there. To this day, after all this time in India, to this day there is a fear that wells up within me. Of course, then there is the realization I have, the certainty that God is greater than all of this. But still, there is such a demonic atmosphere that, if I'm caught in the midst of that group, it is fearful to me, to this day. And I would be dishonest if I said it wasn't. There's a fearfulness, but I do plead the blood of Christ and the power of God that is within me.

DB: *"Greater is He that is in you than he that is in the world"* (1 John 4:4).

Bill: Yes. His word on that is sure, and it's always there. You need that if you get into some of these bad situations, such as the worship of Kali, a very evil goddess popular in the eastern part of India.

DB: When you said people there are worshipping Satan, do you mean Satan as such, or is he called some other name?

Bill: Of course, in each language there's a different name. But it's the chief god or goddess of power, the chief, the one above all of the demons, and that prince of demons is, of course, Satan. They actually call him the god of the power of evil.

DB: So they recognize the difference between spirits of good and spirits of evil?

Bill: Oh, yes. They do have that understanding. It's like the difference we mean when we speak of black magic and white magic. They have that. And they can bring the powers of evil upon others. Very often in these communities, it seems like they work under the assumption that the powers of evil are greater than the powers of good, stronger, because they see that power in destruction, in death, in everything that's happening. And that's where we come in. Of course, I would like to…

Maybe this would be a good time to move into what's happening. I'll be jumping ahead about thirty-five years, cutting out a whole segment of ministry.

DB: That's all right; we can always go back and catch up.

Bill: I'm bringing you up to where we are now. As we have seen what God is doing in India today, I don't think there is any doubt that anyone who was even half-objectively doing a survey in India today could deny this truth: One of the strongest methods that God is using in India to build His church is by demonstrating, in a very dramatic way, that those who are believers in God through Christ have a power that is much greater than any of the powers in the villages or districts where we're located.

DB: That's something that will challenge many Americans, for many still believe that the power God exercised through the Holy Spirit in the days of the early church can't happen today.

Bill: It challenges us, too. And it challenges the Hindus and the worshippers of other gods in India, because they believe that the powers they worship are greater. You can't just go in there having this as a theory. You can't go in and say, "Here is what the Bible says." They will say, "Here is what our spirit does now. What does God's Spirit do?"

It's challenging, and God is demonstrating His power through healings. Joyce and I have also seen satanic healings. I don't know whether that's too evident here in the West or not, but it is in India. It may be here, too. But it certainly is in India. We have seen satanic healings. But there is a clear difference.

Now I'll backtrack. Even in the time when I first came to India, I had no difficulty in acknowledging the power of the Holy Spirit and of evil spirits. I was preaching during our early days almost every Friday night in Secunderabad, at the YMCA. We had meetings every Friday night, but I wasn't always the preacher. These messages were reported in the local secular newspaper. They sent a reporter to every meeting, and he gave two or three columns to a synopsis of the messages that were given in these Friday meetings. So my name was known in the area of Secunderabad and Hyderabad, by virtue of that reporting.

One time a Roman Catholic came to my meeting and challenged me afterward. He said, "I'd like to talk to you. I give mantras. Do you know what mantras are?"

I said, "Yes, I know what mantras are. They're Hindu chanting, prayers to demonic powers for healing."

He said, "I preach the mantra."

Even though he was Roman Catholic! I asked him, "Oh? What happened to you? How did that happen?"

He said, "I had a Hindu friend who was a priest. Anyone bitten by a snake would phone him. He would give the mantra, and almost every time the person would be healed within a few hours. He dealt with other sicknesses, too. Hindu priests are often called in. But this particular priest specialized in healing snake bites through mantras." Then this Roman

Catholic said, "This Hindu, before he died, gave me the mantra, and the power of the mantra by the laying on of hands. I have that power."

I said, "What is the secret of receiving that power?"

He said, "I can't tell you."

I said, "I know you can't. It's a secret thing."

I was trying to draw him out. And he said, "Yes, it's secret." Of course, he tells mantras that others can say, but how he received the power, he was keeping a secret.

He said, "People get cured." Then he challenged me. He said, "Now, you tell me. A person that's bitten by a cobra phones me, and I give them the mantra. One hour later they're calling me and saying, 'Thank you, I'm healed.'" He said, "Can you say that's bad?"

I responded, "Healing someone is not bad. No one would say that healing someone is bad, but what you are doing is bad."

He asked, "Why?"

I said, "I'll tell you why. You are doing something that is imitating a healing far greater than that: a healing that only God can give."

"What do you mean, far greater?"

I said, "God will speak first to the healing of the spirit. Remember when Jesus said to the paralyzed man: 'Son, your sins are forgiven you.' You do not do that."

He said, "No, I can't do that."

I said, "I know you can't. You haven't got the power to do that. God will speak to the spirit; God will speak to the soul, the mind, healing emotional hurts that may have come, even through that sickness, if it's a long-term cancer, or even a snake bite. God will heal that trauma."

I continued, "God can heal the physical also, but in the eyes of God, that is the least important. You're starting at the least important, and you're not going into the most important."

I asked him, "Have you led one person into saving faith, into total life and liberty?"

He said, "No. In fact, most times they're miserable. They're healed, but they're unhappy."

I said, "God will do the healing and make them truly happy in Christ. That's the difference between our God and the mantras that you are doing. You're healing a physical thing, but not touching the real person, which is the spirit and the soul."

He said, "Well, I haven't looked at it like that."

I said, "That's the preaching I'm doing."

I'm sharing this incident, this whole conversation, to make it quite clear that we are confronted. This was a confrontation, when he said, "Do you have something better? I can tell a person bitten by a snake, 'Get up and walk,' through a mantra. Can you do that?" I said, "Yes, we can, but God will deal with something more than that. And even if they don't get up and walk, that's really unimportant because they're eternally saved. I would rather see that happen than them getting up and walking. But, it is possible to do the whole thing, you know, right the whole way through." In the villages, we're seeing this happening again and again—God moving in amazing ways.

Now I'm getting into an area where I could go into story after story. I'll just share one or two.

Joyce: Let me add something here. In acknowledging that these Hindus take these mantras and use them and chant them like prayers—that's how they use them—an interesting part of this is that when people today want mantras for some particular type of situation, they may go to a Muslim priest. Sometimes it's not even a priest, but there will be one particular person in that community who seems to be the master of this type of mantra. Hindus or Parsees or Muslims themselves will go to this man, and pay him to give them a mantra for that particular situation.

Many times they'll put a cord around their wrist, or around their neck, to indicate that they have a certain kind of mantra. Or it may be a little copper scroll that has the mantra on it. Sometimes they put it around their waist as well. Many people do this, and it definitely is an indication of an evil bondage. We have some amazing stories about cutting those cords and what happened as a result.

But going back to the mantras, the story is this. There was one particular railroad station master who was a Christian, and he was very disturbed in his spirit by having to relay a message from this mantra man in Secunderabad, out to the city sixty miles away, through the train station there. When anybody would get a snake bite, and that's usually what a lot of this was, they would carry the person to the rail station, and then have the rail station wire to this man, who was at the rail station in Secunderabad. The "priest" would give the prayer to that station master, who would send it to him. And this Christian stationmaster had to do this because the villagers are not allowed to use the railroad's communication system.

Well this was bothering him terribly. So he went to the Lord, and he prayed, "Lord Jesus, this is happening, and the devil is manifesting his power. Lord, I just ask you to give me the power to do the same thing in Jesus' name." So when people came to him saying, "Call in," he began to say, "No, we're going to consult somebody else." So he began to pray. He would rebuke the poison in the body and claim the healing from the snakebite in Jesus' name.

People were being healed from these things and the glory then was going to Jesus, and not to the evil power, you know, to Satan. So Christians have been reacting to the challenges of the evil powers and finally catching on to the fact that God is greater. That Christian stationmaster became quite well known.

Bill: What's more, he was a traditional believer. He was from a traditional denomination, not a Pentecostal. That's a beautiful illustration. And that's a relatively quiet example. And that is what is happening.

As I said, today we're seeing an explosion in evangelism and church planting, through this power, the release of power, through the signs and wonders that God is doing in India.

DB: When I was invited by Bernie May to spend a couple

of days at a base the Wycliffe Bible Translators have in Arlington, Texas, I heard wonderful stories of how God is doing this same kind of thing in many parts of the world, amazing stories. It's not unusual to hear stories of the power of the Holy Spirit on what we call "the mission field." But in America such stories are suspect. We don't see many signs and wonders, and some that have been claimed have been proved to be fraudulent. I often wonder whether we see so few miracles here because we expect few. I wonder if America is perhaps something like a modern Capernaum. The Bible tells us that Jesus Himself could do no mighty works there because of their unbelief.

Bill: Let me tell you about the time some students came to me while I was on furlough in America once, doing deputation work, which simply means stirring up support for missions. These students asked me to come and pray with them and for them.

Well, I was brought up Irish Baptist, and that did not include any of this charismatic business, but I guess these kids assumed I was filled with the Spirit.

They came to me and said, "We want you to pray for us."

Well, of course, ministers pray for kids, so I agreed.

One of them said, "I'm into drugs, pray." And I prayed a pretty superficial prayer, "Dear God. You know."

And then they sort of looked at me as if to say, "Hey, you're not real. I wanted to be delivered, but you couldn't come in the power that would say, 'In the name of Jesus, I set you free.'"

I went from that meeting devastated. They didn't see the devastation. They only saw the exuberance that I was showing. But I went back to my motel room, and I was in tears. I prayed, "God, I can't keep on going. You're either going to have to do something in my life to take away this dryness, so that I can speak with authority and power, or I'm going to ask to be stopped doing any kind of deputation work. I can't keep going like this. These kids wanted something tonight that in my training I couldn't give. They wanted Your power released tonight, and I just wasn't there."

I was changed that night. I don't care what kind of terminology you use to describe it, but I was changed, because I cried out for help that night back at the motel. Actually it turned out to be very simple, very simple. I was sitting there, talking to God. I don't think there was an audible voice, but as far as I'm concerned, we were both speaking out loud. I was alone, speaking just like I'm speaking right now. I was crying. I said, "God, I want something. I want this." I knew what the whole thing was, generally. I had done a lot of reading and research about it. "I want this experience." Then I heard God say to me within my spirit, whether it was a voice or just an impression, "Bill, what do you want?"

Well, the Bible says that the Lord wants us to be *"be filled with all the fulness of God"* (Ephesians 3:19) and to *"be filled with the Spirit"* (Ephesians 5:18). So I said, "I want Your fullness; I want to be filled with Your Holy Spirit. I think that's what they are talking about."

He said, "All right, how did you get salvation?"

I thought I should answer, so I took my Bible and notebook and led God into salvation. I opened up to Ephesians 2:8, *"By grace are ye saved through faith; and that not of yourselves; it is the gift of God."*

He said, "What is it?"

"It is the gift of God."

"How do you get a gift?"

"Well, you receive it."

I closed my Bible, I said, "God, I receive it."

I started to thank God, and the tears that were of desperation literally turned into tears of joy.

Then I made a conscious decision. I said, "Now, God, I want to be zapped," and God didn't zap me.

That's what God brought me to. He said, "You're putting all these conditions on it. Just receive the gift. If nothing happens to you, just say, 'Thanks for the gift.'"

I said, "Okay." That's where I came to that night. So I received it. It was not like some of the experiences that others have described. For me it was an act of faith on the basis of the Word of God that I had studied—faith that I now had this—and I used it. It was so simple that I thought, "Why have I been struggling for five or six long years, trying to understand this?" But it was so simple. I'm still dry now at times, but from that day on, whenever it happens, I just say, "Okay, God, I have received your gift."

You see, I've now come to the point where I know that this is what the Bible says. I was not interpreting the Bible the way I was told to interpret it by my Irish Baptists or by any other group. I wasn't taking my thoughts to the Bible to look for something that would prove what I was thinking. I let go of what I had and let the Bible speak to me. When the Bible spoke to me, the Bible said, "You have received God's gift of the filling of the Holy Spirit." I said, "Okay." My Baptists say I haven't, but the Word says I have. "I believe your Word, Lord!" So I ceased being an Irish Baptist and became a Bible-believing child of God. It was as simple as that. I know that we can go into a lot of details, but I've tried to condense it as much as I could.

But let me go on a moment, because what happened after that is very important. After that I had the driest experience in my whole life. I was totally discouraged. Joyce and I were apart, since she had to stay on in the United States. I had brought the kids back to India.

Joyce: Yes. That was in 1972. I had stayed. I had one seminary course to finish, and so I stayed back to do that. He took all four children and went back to India.

Bill: So I left Joyce in America. I went back to India from my furlough after this experience, feeling totally discouraged—not on cloud nine—totally discouraged. "Lord, why have I got to be separated from my wife again for some months? Why must I go to India, separate immediately from my four kids as they go to boarding school, go back to a big old house, and all I have is two dogs and three birds?"

I was sitting in the house, totally discouraged, so much so that it's the only time in my mission experience where I considered stopping being a missionary. I had got a call to two churches while I was in the US on furlough, two Baptist churches. They didn't actually give me a call, but they said, "Bill, would you consider coming if we gave you a call?" That meant that if I said yes, they would definitely bring me in as a pastor. Two churches had asked me, and both of them I had refused. Now, back in India, I sat and said, "God, I think that's your calling. I'm going to go back to one of those churches."

That's how discouraged I was, to the point where I was about to call Joyce and say, "Contact both of those churches. If either say yes, let me know. I'll get the kids, we'll come back, and you don't have to come over here." That's where I was, totally discouraged.

A little later my colleague in India came to see me.

Joyce: I was back by then.

Bill: Yes. And this colleague and I had worked together for years in ministry. We were talking about what we were going to do with the socioeconomic programs that we were involved in. He was the director, and I was the bursar of that ministry.

As we were talking, we had a time of prayer, just as we always did. I mean, we always prayed for what we were going to do afterwards. So we had the time of prayer. At this time of utter discouragement, after we got up from the prayer, this colleague, who knew me well for many years, said, "Bill, what's the matter with you?"

I thought he meant, "You sound so discouraged, and so down." I said, "What do you mean?" He said, "There's a power in your prayer that I have never seen before. Something stirred when you were praying."

Now, I had said nothing. In fact, I was utterly discouraged. But he saw in my prayer, he heard in my prayer, something that in all those years that he knew me he had never seen. And that really touched me. I said, "Oh, God, this is real then!

Something real has happened! He didn't see my discouragement; he saw Your grace and Your love and Your fire and Your power!"

And that, Don, was a confirmation of what I had happened. Really it was an act of faith, accepting from God what He said in His Word. And for me, that's the way I had to come. I had to be convinced that it was right from the Word, not from church and not from people that were talking about it. I had to see that it said it in His Word. Once I got that conviction, then I said, "Okay, God. I believe You, and I accept it." So that's how I came to where I am today.

# The Scott Ministry Album

## Bill's Early Ministry

**Bill visiting a village to preach 1951**

**Our first car purchased in India 1953**

**Bill and Leonard with some school boys — 1951**

# The Scott Ministry Album

## Joyce's Early Ministry

Joyce playing a harmonica to draw a crowd for the Sunday services — 1952

Mr. Steenstra helping Joyce keep score during a quiz on people of the Bible — 1951

Joyce in the lab at the Church of South India Hospital, where she was lab supervisor.

# The Scott Ministry Album

## Bill's Hands-On Approach

**Dedicating another church**

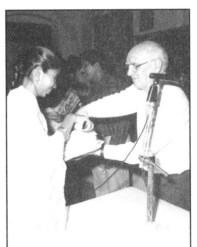

**Handing out the CBS materials to a volunteer teacher**

**Blessing and dedicating some ladies ready to do CBS work**

# The Scott Ministry Album

## Schools of Evangelism

**New bicycles for SOE students**
**Vehicles to reach the unreached**

**SOE graduates in the Extension Course**

# The Scott Ministry Album

## Schools of Evangelism

**Abraham Rai doing door-to-door evangelism**

**First Lambardi convert, Gypsy tribe**

**Na Awk tribe Raja (chief) with Rev. David and missionaries — 1994**

# The Scott Ministry Album

## Schools of Evangelism

**Bill dedicating another new SOE church**

**Witnessing the baptisms — March 14–16, 1989**

Chapter 15
# Schools of Evangelism

**B**ill: As these partnerships and expanded ministries were developing, the churches were beginning to ask, "What's going on?" Our people are out evangelizing, they're out giving tracts, they're distributing books. They never did these things before!" So the pastors were beginning to ask, and then the church presidents and bishops above the pastors were beginning to ask.

So then I thought, well, now it's time. Out of this growth and development came the moment when I felt it was time for us to bring together the top leadership of the churches and tell them about IBL—presidents, bishops, etc.—to tell them about the resources we had to assist work through their churches. Also we wanted to expand our Scripture distribution program. So we were bringing in those who were using the program, plus many who were not, to expose them to what was happening.

So those leaders' conferences had two purposes. They were first inspirational, and then they were informational. And out of the conferences, we wanted them to act. We wanted to inspire them to do something for God in India, and we wanted to inform them how they could do something with the resources that IBL has. They were five-day conferences where we gave Bible messages of inspiration, where we put on sessions of information, and where we had sharing by others.

After the top levels, then we brought in the mid-level, the pastors under whom there would be a number of Bible women and evangelists. We informed them and inspired them and asked them to get involved. Finally we brought in the field level, the people, the Bible women, the evangelists. So that was the origin of the conferences.

Why did we have conferences and seminars? It wasn't just to have a conference or to have a seminar, but it was because now we were expanding, and people needed both inspiration and information. So we had these on a yearly basis, where they would come back again and again to get fired up for God, to be inspired, and then also to be informed about any new programs and resources.

DB: And that, then, is what made possible the expansion from two or three thousand Bibles a year to seventy thousand pieces each working day?

Bill: That's right. After that in that framework comes the School of Evangelism, SOE, which is more concentrated and focused. It's not so much a training program as an equipping program: equipping evangelists to be frontline evangelists. We talked it over and developed the ideas as the conferences grew. Then we got the churches to identify evangelists, men who were already doing the work of evangelism. Our School of Evangelism is for them, to train and equip them for pioneer work in the villages.

Bill Teate: I never knew that; for years, I never knew it.

Bill: Yes, it's for evangelists, and we bring in evangelists. We're doing another development, which is what you were thinking about, Bill, but this was for evangelists. Then we asked these churches to release these evangelists from doing their regular work of evangelism to go into frontline evangelism, places where there is no church. That's why we sponsor them for a year. We don't pay their salary, but we sponsor them to enable the church to release them from their regular responsibilities into this frontline work, and then we equip them to do that, which is a very different kind of work.

So they're already evangelists. They've already got some experience, or at least they're already called. Some may only have been evangelists for three months, some for thirty years. But they're evangelists, you know. They don't come in cold, as non-evangelists, to be trained in evangelism. They are evangelists already, and they come to be equipped to do frontline evangelism. It's all about getting God's Word to the villages.

They're sponsored for a year. There's one month of teaching and three months in the field; one month of teaching, three months in the field; one month of teaching, three months field. In the first month of teaching, there's strong Bible emphasis. There's a hundred hours of Bible, so that's strong Bible teaching. We also emphasize evangelism, and expose them to what God is doing in evangelism in India.

Joyce: All kinds of evangelism.

Bill: The second session of classroom work we emphasize discipling, helping new believers to grow. We bring in those who are experienced in this. Then in the third session, we emphasize the teaching of the Word: the teaching of the Word and the establishing of a recognized church, a church recognized by the government as well as by their own church body. So those are the three month-long teaching sessions that we have, and the nine months of field work, out doing what they have been taught.

Bill Teate: After the first month of class work, they go out and do jail evangelism, things like that.

Joyce: Or just village evangelism, child evangelism, whatever. Then they come back. The second academic month that they're there, we teach them how to be disciplers of those they have won, establishing them, teaching them, and bringing them to maturity in the Christian life.

Bill Teate: With group study and things like that.

Joyce: Right, whatever way the student feels would be best. Then he comes back for his third academic month, and finally out for those last three months to establish the churches.

Bill Teate: They are called Schools of Evangelism in India; here in America we call them church planting schools, because we want the churches here to know that we are really giving them the opportunity to train church planters.

Bill: There was a conflict about the name. Another ministry

was already using the name "Church Planters," so we called ours Schools of Evangelism. Even prior to SOE, there were many conferences at which we were bringing pastors and evangelists together, and this is the development that Don is asking about, because now we were distributing Scriptures, now we were working through the churches, now we were mobilizing people within the churches.

It is interesting, because, again, it's only in retrospect that we can see clearly what God has done. In working for God, you don't always realize what's happening as it is happening.

I was having these conversations with various church groups in India at many levels. Then I had a visit with John DeVries, who had just joined the World Home Bible League. They had made me Director for India, and so every time John came to India, he and I would sit down and talk. He is a man of ideas.

On one of these visits, John and I were sitting, talking and strategizing, when he came up with an idea, "Bill, what would you think of having a school?" This was in 1984, and we were sitting in a hotel room, having a cup of coffee. John asked, "What would you think of establishing schools to train evangelists?"

I immediately reacted positively, and John knew that if I did, something was going to happen. We knew each other pretty well by then. He wanted to establish a school, and I said, "Well, we bring in twelve evangelists, and we'll have a class in the north, in our office in the north, and we'll have a class in the south." So we brought in twenty-four people to train as evangelists.

Very quickly I saw that that was wrong; we had made a mistake. I told John, "We mustn't bring these men in from the villages to the city, to facilities that they know nothing about. None of them has seen running water from a spigot. None of them has used a toilet in his life; they just use the fields. We're bringing them into a culture that is almost completely un-known to them. They don't even like the city food. They're uncomfortable. They won't learn how to be good evangelists here." So I said, "We've made a mistake. We will take the school to them."

That's when I developed what we called the On-Site School of Evangelism. Another change we made was a decision not to bring in raw people and try to turn them into evangelists. That came out of the first class, too. I realized that in a three-month training program, or even in a year, we're not going to train non-evangelists to become evangelists. It just isn't going to work. So I said, "We'll bring in men who are already evangelists and equip them, equip them to do the job of evangelism in unreached areas."

I've condensed what happened over a couple of years into a couple of paragraphs. But that was how the concept developed.

Now it has grown from those two classes, twelve men in each, in two cities, to a hundred classes that are now equipping twelve hundred motivated evangelists all over India. And the classes are on-site.

**DB:** The original two classes were in 1984?

**Bill:** Yes. And in 1985 we trained forty evangelists. In 1986 it was roughly sixty, and in the third year, 1987, it was roughly eighty. By 1993, the number was up to 300 SOE students. And then a couple of years ago we hit a thousand, and now it's up to twelve hundred.

**Bill Teate:** Tell about the financing of the schools, Bill, since you have always been so concerned about following the principle God gave you to make sure that money would not control ministry.

**Bill:** Well, I again insisted that there be no direct funding of this school, and that the funding would come through the sale of Bibles. To get back to the beginning when this idea was shared and we were strategizing, one of the reasons I was excited about the whole idea of a School of Evangelism was because my primary vision has always been getting the Word of God into the hands of the people of India. I immediately saw an opportunity to get literally hundreds of thousands more Bibles into India, and out of the funds coming back from those Bibles, this ministry would be done. So that's how it is funded to this day.

Bill Teate: For the fourteen years that I have promoted the work here in America, inviting churches here to participate, I've always been able to say, "If you give money for SOE, which I call church planting school, your money will be used twice. It's always put first into Bibles, and then from the sale of those Bibles, at prices that make them very affordable to the people of the villages, that money is then used a second time, to train the church planters.

Bill: Yes, and I want to emphasize what Bill has said. It's so exciting to me, because when a person gives, the money gets the Bibles into India, into the hands of people who pay for them and who read them, not to people who get them free and sell them for waste paper. That in itself is a tremendous, mighty, effective ministry for God. But then they're getting an extra benefit, a secondary one, which is that they're going to train a student, or a class of students, with funding that comes from the sale of those Bibles.

Another exciting part of this story is the various ways God is raising the support for this ministry from within India. Today, even if all foreign funding for this ceased, it would only decrease the present program 40%, because 60% comes from India.

DB: And that Indian funding comes from Indian churches?

Bill: Right, Indian churches and Indian missions.

Bill Teate: When it started, it depended on foreign sources for 90% of the funding, right, Bill? And 10% came from India?

Bill: Yes, that 10% has now grown to 60%, and our goal is that the whole SOE program will be totally funded from within India before too long.

DB: At its present level?

Bill: Yes, at its present level, and that to me is exciting. It's exciting to have a program that the church in India is willing to look at and say, "We need it! We see the need so clearly that we are willing to pay the cost!" That's exciting.

There has always been a cost to the Indian churches, by the way. This was never a handout program even on day one. From the beginning, we gave what we could give, but the Indian church also had to give. We gave a stipend, not a salary.

For every evangelist that an Indian church released to this program, the church were responsible for half of his salary. The evangelist was paid completely by the church he came from, not by us. We gave the funds to the church, and they kept those evangelists on their payroll. The men were responsible to their church, and the church was responsible to us only in that they had to report what those men were doing. Then we gave that information back to the supporters and sponsors from outside India.

DB: Bill, that sounds as though the men going through training as church planters in the School of Evangelism might not even know that any foreign money was involved. They would see their support as coming from that mother church in India.

Bill: That was the arrangement. And that's the reason we set it up that way, because these evangelists are village evangelists. They do not know the structure of funding. They know that there is an indigenous organization called India Bible Literature; they come to our conferences. And they know that this organization, staffed with Indians, all paid from Indian funds, is partnering with them, and they're still getting their salary from their church. Only the church knows that we're sponsoring the student.

We don't use the word "support." We *invest* in the life of nationals, and an investment always gives a return. So I use the word "invest." Rather than support nationals, I say *we partner with nationals. So* it's a partnership of investment: their lives and our resources coming together to launch their ministry, and that results in eternal returns, returns for the rest of time, results that will be in eternity.

DB: It sounds a lot like the difference between a parent's supporting a son all his life, and a parent's investing in him by putting him through college so that he can support himself for life.

Bill: Yes. Also, when we do things that way, the evangelist is not in any way detached or alienated. His ties and link with his church are not in any way broken. In fact they are strengthened.

DB: Let me ask you something else. Why did Indian ministries and missions not put more Bibles out before you started distributing Bibles? The translations had already been done, and I'm sure that anyone who wanted to buy Bibles in India for distribution could have found them. How did India Bible Literature make a difference?

Bill: There's just so much, I don't like to say it, but there is so much corruption. That's what the Indian evangelists were disgusted with. This is where the corruption comes through. When some of the suppliers of Bibles would get an advance of 300,000 or 400,000 rupees, they would invest that, but they would take out the interest for themselves. Then, after six months, they would cash in the investment, and then the Bibles would be supplied, but they've had six months of interest that they would keep. That made the Indian evangelists angry.

We don't do that. We don't even take any money until our customers have the books in their hands. We refuse to take it any faster. They know that. In fact, sometimes we supply the Bibles, and they send the money afterwards. So that is the reason why many more come to us. It's not that the other suppliers don't have them. They have Bibles, but some of them sometimes want to get or keep or work up some float, or graft, or whatever it is. And that's what makes people angry: they know the Bibles, or New Testaments, are sitting there. The organization often won't let them out because their heart is not in evangelism; their heart is in getting some money, whatever way they can.

DB: Let me ask something else on that subject, since the giving of Bibles is the basic way in which Christians outside India can participate in all this ministry. What does it cost to give a Bible in India? You say that people in America are your partners, giving you Bibles. What are they getting for their gifts? If I wanted to give a hundred dollars, how many Bibles would that buy in India?

Bill: It depends on the language we're talking about. India is a multilingual nation, and a Telugu Bible is half the size of a Bengali Bible. That makes the Bengali Bible twice the cost of the Telugu Bible. So it's hard to say. I come up with an average cost, of $2.00 to $2.50 per Bible. That's average. Some would cost less than that to print, some would cost more than that. So that's an average cost for us to print a Bible. If we buy it from Bible Society or some other mission organization that has put in a subsidy, then of course we get it at a lower cost.

DB: Then you take the Bibles that you have either bought or printed and get those into the hands of the people of India. And out of the money you get for them, you maintain your building and your organization and all of these ministries?

Bill: And the ministries. That's right. The money works twice, at least twice. It trains them and equips them to be self-supporting and to make them master church planters, who in turn are training Timothys. You've got an investment for life; you've got an investment that's going to continue to give returns. It's an investment.

DB: So any money from America pays for Scriptures? And the money you get from distributing the Scriptures goes into programs of equipping church planters who are self-supporting, plus into Jesus-based literacy training, and into other programs? And none of the foreign money pays for the ongoing support of the church workers?

Bill: That's right.

DB: That's impressive.

# Chapter 16

# "From Whence Cometh My Help?"

**D**B: I remember hearing my father talk often about the issues of self-support versus foreign money after his sixteen-month long tour of missions in the 1930s. He said he found that missions had often made the mistake of creating a culture of dependency. He talked about the scandals and problems that resulted from what were called "rice Christians" in China.

It seems that with all the goodwill in the world, moved by the same kind of generous impulses that fashioned the welfare system in the United States, missions have sometimes fostered conditions that have distorted many of the key aspects of the gospel message, and at the same time damaged relationships with the nations sending the missionaries. The parallels with the welfare system are not perfect, but some apply. When new Christians in the nations receiving missionaries are conditioned to depend on foreign money, they do not learn to rely on God for direction and power. I asked Bill Scott to comment.

Bill, I have noticed the emphasis you put on the principle of self-support for the ministry programs you have developed. Has there been any difficulty persuading people in India to accept your thinking about this?

Bill: We've had to face the issue a number of times, and out of the many times that this has happened, I'll talk about just one, one of the earlier occasions, and share it with you as an example of what has happened over and over through the years.

## "From Whence Cometh My Help?"

This happened in the early 1970s, when we were just beginning to expand the ministry. I had a conference in Calcutta with a group of Indian church leaders—I can't remember the exact number, about fifteen or twenty. They were leaders from different states of northeast India, and the west and the surrounding states. I was there sharing the vision and the burden of starting the work of evangelism and the church planting on a very large scale and wanting the churches to become self-supporting.

I could see that a number of these leaders were not fully in agreement. Their eyebrows were going up, and they were looking at me strangely. So I said, "I can see that some of you have got questions in your minds. Okay. We're Indians. What is the problem?"

I said that because I was the only non-Indian there, and they accepted me as one of them. I had been in India over twenty years at that time.

They said, "It won't work."

"What do you mean, it won't work? Why not?"

They said, "We're too poor. The Indian church is too poor."

Now the people that were talking were people that had traveled. They had visited America and other western countries frequently, and they were getting support funds from those countries for pastors and for evangelists. They were the ones that were talking.

I said, "Look, we are not a poor nation." I was speaking as an Indian. I knew a number of them, and I said, "Let me ask you something. You came to Christ as Hindus. You used to be Hindus; then you came to Christ. Right?"

They said, "Yes."

I said, "As Hindus, did you go to the temple?"

"Oh, yes, regularly, we worshipped every day. We went to the temple periodically and went to the sacred places periodically."

I said, "Did you ever once go to the temple without a gift

to your gods?"

They said, "Never. That would be an insult to the gods."

I said, "You brought flowers, you brought fruit, you brought money. Right?"

They said, "Yes."

I should explain also that if you were in India, when you became a Christian, you stopped the habits of smoking, drinking, and gambling. That was just the effect of it. When you became a Christian, those things stopped. So I went on down through those three things.

I said, "Before you were a Christian, before God saved you, did you smoke?"

They said, "Yes, we smoked."

"How much did you spend?"

They told me.

"How much did you spend on movies?"

They told me.

"How much did you spend in gambling?"

They told me.

"How much did you spend on women, wine?"

They told me. Because those things were part of their lifestyle that they lived as non-Christians.

I said, "Now God has saved you. You're freed from all those destructive habits that were ruining your life. You've got that money, and you've got the temple money, what you used to spend on the temples. The temple money alone comes to more than a thousand rupees per year, according to the government of India. Now you've got that to give to God. Are you telling me that the God you now worship is less worthy than the Hindu gods to receive your money and gifts?"

They said, "But we've never heard this before."

I said, "But that's the teaching of the Bible. You start giving to God."

After the time of that conference, a couple of them came and said to me, "We've stopped the business of looking to the West for money. We now tell our people 'We give to God.'"

What I said to them that day I've said again and again to others. I've challenged people to give to God at least the money that they've saved through becoming a Christian. "Give at least that. I think you should give more than that, but give at least that. And if you do, our churches will be self-supporting from day one."

DB: What is a thousand rupees in American money?

Bill: At that exchange rate then, it was about $120. But a thousand rupees a year was a figure that was given back around 1970. That figure has probably gone up now; it's probably four to five times that now. But that was a government figure of the average individual's giving to a temple.

DB: In addition, they would have the money they save from the change of habits?

Bill: Change of lifestyle and habits. So if you get ten people giving a thousand rupees a year, you've got enough to support a pastor in India, not by American standards but by Indian standards. You get a pastor who gets a salary of five or six hundred rupees per month—that's his salary per month. And, if they give them gifts in kind, you cut down that monetary need. They give them a house equivalent to what they're living in, and that house might be worth 30, 40, 50 rupees per month. So you see, you've got a pastor.

But what happens when you have support from the West is that you bring the pastor to a living standard that is far beyond the living standard of his parishioners. Then they're not going to listen to him. He's not going to be able to counsel them. He won't be able to say, "You're in need, and I know it." They're going to say, "You know nothing about me. You're living in a mansion. You've got a fortune. You get in a month what we earn in a year."

So I challenge leaders there. I say, "We are Indians. Let us live as Indians, not as Westerners."

As I said, out of that conference a couple of the leading men came and said, "We needed to hear that. Why didn't our missionaries teach us this?"

I said, "I don't know."

But they kept saying, "Why didn't someone tell us this? We were taught, when you're Christians, you get."

I said, "The Bible teaches that when you're Christians, you give. And in your missing that giving, we've denied you a blessing. The blessing we've denied you is the blessing of giving, because the Bible says, *'It is more blessed to give than to receive'* (Acts 20:35). We have denied you the blessing of giving. And I don't want to do that!"

They said, "Thank you!"

I said, "I want you to be blessed, so give!"

**Bill Teate:** When we were having lunch earlier today, Bill told me that this is still an issue. He was recently in a meeting where there were Indians, and they said, "We don't believe this could work." But, of course, it is, in fact, working.

I know also that just a little over a year ago I was sitting in a meeting at a very large church in California with the missions pastor; he invited two Indians in to listen to what I had to say, to check his judgment on whether what I was saying was right or not. When I told about the self-support dimension, both of those Indians said, "That's impossible. That can't be working."

I said, "Well, I know that it is." Then I said nothing more, because the Americans always listen to Indians rather than an American. But I wished Bill had been there, so that he could tell them and give more details. Some Indians here will still say, "That can't work; it's impossible."

**Bill:** But of course it has worked, over and over, and it is working all the time.

**DB:** Bill, your principles remind me of a book my Dad had in his library, *Missionary Methods: Saint Paul's or Ours?* by Roland Allen. Are you familiar with that book?

**Bill:** Yes, very much. In fact, at Bible College in Scotland that was one of the textbooks in our missions class. It must have had a real effect on me. I didn't realize how much of an effect it had on my life until recently. Now when I read it, I the thought suddenly comes to me, "Hey, Roland Allen, he's writing what I'm doing!" As I said, to my knowledge, I didn't read these books to imitate what was there. But the ideas just got into my subconscious and into my spirit, and then the Spirit quickened that and it came out in Bill Scott's way. So I thank God for men of God like Roland Allen.

Joyce: We had that book also in Bible College. Was he English or was he Irish, Scotch?

Bill: He was British, and he worked in India.

# Chapter 17
# The Building

**D**B: There is a very familiar difference between giving a man a fish and teaching him to fish. The first feeds him for a day, and teaches him dependence. The second feeds him for life, and teaches him independence.

For similar reasons, Bill and Joyce Scott have long recognized the difference between what kind of outside support for Christian ministry in India was helpful, and what kind was not. They have accepted partnership from churches outside India to train and equip evangelists, but not to pay evangelists.

Sometimes the Indian Christians are even encouraged to help themselves with capital costs, shouldering part of the investment when it would have been easy to justify accepting all the money from overseas. That happened in connection with the very remarkable story of the building that is the headquarters of the Scotts' India Bible Literature operation, an operation that now distributes 70,000 pieces of Christian literature a day.

Bill: The building was just completed January 19, 1994. And this was, actually, God's doing. I was against putting any money into bricks and mortar, against having any kind of a building, and God in His way brought me to a point where I was willing. I won't go into the details of that except that God changed my mind and brought me into what was, for IBL, His purposes, namely, to put up a building.

DB: You said for IBL?

Bill: India Bible Literature. So we decided at that point that we would trust God to supply the needs for this building in two ways. From our overseas partners we would look to God to supply through them the funds that were needed to buy the ground, the property that was needed. That was about $300,000. Also, we would trust our Indian partners to put up the building, which was again about $300,000 for a two-story building. That will give you an idea of how much farther money goes in India than in the United States.

That was what we left before God and before our staff, and that's what happened. We got the money from overseas to buy the ground. Then thousands of people from India came and gave gifts, which enabled us to put up two stories, the ground floor and the first story as we call it in India, or the first and the second as they are known in America.

While this building was going up, Joyce got a burden that she shared with me: "What about putting a third story on, which could be a literacy center for the training of literacy teachers for all of India?" I said, "I think that's a good vision, and we'll go with it as God supplies."

This was confirmed in a very beautiful way because a friend of ours in India whom we had known for many years came into Joyce's office and said to her, not knowing what we were thinking, "Why don't you put on a third story for a literacy training center?" Joyce had tears in her eyes; she lifted the intercom and called me, still with tears, and said, "Bill, you won't believe what has happened. Our friend, John David, has said the same thing." I simply replied, "Well, that's God's confirmation." But this friend went beyond just saying it. He said, "In order for you to do it, I'm giving the first gift," and he gave us a gift of the equivalent of almost $25,000 from his organization for us to do this.

DB: American or Indian?

Bill: This is an Indian.

Joyce: He was an evangelist who had no backing himself.

Bill: And he gave us the equivalent of nearly $25,000. He said, "That will come to you by post tomorrow, the draft will come," and it did. Over 600,000 rupees.

DB: How did you get to know this man?

Bill: We had known John David, this brother, for many years.

**Joyce:** Since 1965.

**Bill:** Since 1965, when he was beginning his ministry. When we were struggling in our ministry, he was living in a village, and we were living in another village. He often came through our village and stopped in our home. He has frequently told us, "Yours was the home that was truly a home. You would feed me, you would share the meals you were eating." That to him was a blessing. He became just like a part of our family.

We were not in close contact for a number of years prior to this last meeting, when we went to Madras. We hadn't seen him often, but we were praying for him, and he was praying for us. Meanwhile, his ministry built up, our ministry built up, and that's when he came into the scene, talking about this all-India literacy center.

So we got this $25,000. We had the money for the two floors already. So I told the architect and the contractor, "Start on the third floor, but we've only got enough for one third of that floor." It would take about $75,000 more to build that whole area. "We've got $25,000. You do one third," and I showed them the area on the plans. "You do up to there, put a partition, and stop."

He said, "No, we'll trust you."

But I said, "That's all the money we have. We're trusting God, and if God doesn't give it, then that's all that God wants us to do."

Meanwhile, I had bankers coming into my office from all the banks that we used in India, Indian bankers, and they were pleading with me to take a loan.

They wanted to give me a loan. I said, "No, thank you. I appreciate your offering this, but I don't want to take a loan."

They even said, "We'll make it very low terms. You can pay over many years if you wish." They were giving me all the best terms that they could.

And I said, "No, thank you."

Our supporters in India, many among them, came and

said, "We will take out our savings from the bank, give it to you interest free. You may pay it back as and when you can."

I had that offer if I'd wanted to take it. But I still wasn't at peace; that was still borrowing. I said to God, "We don't want to go into debt for this." So the architect and the contractor started to build the one-third that I said to build.

Joyce: But he went on building; he didn't listen to Bill. He heard Bill, and he said, "Okay, okay," but when he started to build, he built the whole floor. He's a Christian man, a Spirit-filled man, but just in faith, he said, "I believe God will do this." He's an Indian, too. He just started to build the whole thing, without our knowing that.

DB: So you were not around? You were in a different part of India at this time?

Joyce: That's right. We did not know he was doing that; we thought he was doing what Bill told him. On his own, by faith, he began to do the whole thing.

Bill: When I saw it, I said, "What are you doing?"

He told us, "I'm going to build it all. I'll trust God with you for the supply of the need. Whenever you get the money, you pay me." It turned out that as he was building, the money came in, and we were able to pay him fully when he completed that third story. It is a building in India that the Indians call "our building," and it truly is their building, given by God.

I've been sharing this story with churches, challenging them, because there is an element of fear that often intrudes when we need to trust God. Trusting goes beyond what we can know in the flesh. Trusting often goes beyond what I would say is really reasonable, judging simply by my training and ex-perience as an accountant.

But you just trust for that extra, as long as you know it's what God wants you to do. I thought, "If God wants to give us one-third of the top story, He'll give one-third. If He wants to give us two-thirds, He'll give two. If He wants to give us the whole top story, he'll give it." And He did.

DB: I remember you told us about your training as an

accountant in Britain, but you have other training also, right?

Bill: Yes, I have a hospital administration diploma from Indiana University. Later I also did some studies at Wharton School of Business at the University of Pennsylvania.

DB: I'm curious about a couple of things. You mentioned that the builder was a Christian. Do you know his story?

Joyce: He's an Assemblies of God man, and belongs to a large Assemblies of God church there in Madras. But how he became a Christian, I don't know.

DB: This building is in Madras?

Joyce: Yes, it's in Madras. Some people say, "You mean these Indians did all this?" That's the miracle in this. Yes, the Indians gave so that that building could be in existence. The only reason they gave is because God has used IBL from the north of India to the south, east, and west, and people have been blessed by it. Therefore, they have given. Otherwise, they would not give. Indians are very conservative in their giving.

DB: And India Bible Literature covers all the different languages of India, or at least the major ones? I've heard a great deal about how India is fragmented into more than a dozen major language groups. Do you manage to cover them all?

Joyce: Yes. A few years ago the government increased the official number of major languages to include some of those that we used to call tribal. Officially there were sixteen major languages until about a year or two ago, and they've increased it, I think, by about four or five.

DB: And by a "major" language group we mean that at least ten million people speak it?

Joyce: Yes, major would mean at least ten million. For example, the Gujarati people have their own language. That's in an area north of Bombay. The Marathi people include Bombay. The Hindi belt is all up north. Down south the Tamil people have their own language. There are 63 million people that speak Telugu. Then there are also, let's see, there are so many I probably can't call them all off. But starting from South India, there's Tamil, Malayalam, Kannada, Telugu, Marathi, Hindi,

Oriya, and then we get Bengali, and come across to Gujarati, Punjabi, Urdu, and then we have, in the northeast of India, Manipuri and Assamese… How many is that?

DB: I get the point!

Joyce: All together there are over 800 languages and dialects in India. Those are major ones. When it comes down to it, India is a nation of bilingual communities.

DB: So many factors to divide people! You know, some Americans will be surprised that the builder who had such enthusiasm for your project and worked so closely with you was in the Assemblies of God, and was still quite happy working with you even though you are Baptist.

Joyce: Oh yes, but we don't talk about being Baptist. We just love Jesus over there.

DB: And all the various denominations work with you?

Joyce: India Bible Literature is interdenominational in every way. We work with churches, with parachurch organizations, with church service agencies, all sorts.

Bill: This is true even in our staff. In our five offices, what would you say that our direct staff is, roughly?

Joyce: Direct staff? I think we've got about one hundred and eighty.

Bill: And these staff in our organization actually reflect the outreach of India Bible Literature, because in our staff we have those from the traditional denominations such as Presbyterian, Methodist, and Baptist, and then we have those from Pentecostal denominations like the Assemblies of God, Church of God, Church of Christ, those major denominations,…

Joyce: Seventh Day Adventists, Catholic …

Bill: And then we have those who are independent, various types of assemblies, and independent Pentecostal fellowships, and they're working together, day after day.

DB: All on staff?

Bill: All on staff.

DB: Anybody from the Church of South India?

Bill: Yes, and the Church of North India, and Nazarene.

Our staff really is a fellowship of all the churches, and they are reaching out.

But to backtrack a bit, about this building, we've always lived with the philosophy that the purpose of our being in India is to minister, not to build up an organization. So we built a ministry that supports the organization, and not the other way around. Without the ministry, the organization would collapse. So we don't have an organization that is there and being supported by funds, but we have a ministry that is being supported by funds, and out of that, the organization is supported.

And in terms of building, I have a very strong feeling that the resources God gives to us are resources to be invested in people and not invested in brick and mortar unless the brick and mortar are necessary to serve the people and the ministry, and that's what happened with this building.

To finish up the story on the building, we were paying to rent space before we built the new building. If we now had to rent the space we have built, we would be paying out enough money in rent to have equipped about 100 frontline church planters. So now we've had funds to do that, and we have the building, too.

DB: How much were you paying in rent?

Bill: In rupees, it would be about 75,000 rupees per month, which would be about $2,500 a month.

DB: Ordinarily we might say that in six years your building paid for itself, but we normally say that when we think about paying off a mortgage, paying off borrowed money. In this case you borrowed nothing. It seems the rent money you saved went directly into ministry instead; is that right? There was no one to pay back. So you were able to train and equip more evangelists to work in the villages?

Bill: That's right. We were equipping our frontline evangelists through the school of evangelism, and that's what made me happy about this. People who gave to put up this building, both our partners abroad and in India, were really investing in lives by releasing us from the payment of rent.

# The Building

And I'm not rationalizing the putting up of the building; I'm only saying that within my own spirit, I was able, once we got into this, to be happy about it because of the release of funds for ministry.

DB: It costs 10,000 rupees to put a man through your School of Evangelism, so you could put about ninety men through each year on the money you save by not having to pay rent.

Bill: Yes. And that equips the man properly, with literature and all the rest. So in six years we saved enough to put over five hundred frontline evangelists out in the villages, fully trained and fully equipped.

# Chapter 18

# "Let the Little Children Come"

**B**ill: This is a kind of flashback, but I must tell you. One day Krupanidhi came to me and said, "We've got a children's book." Somehow or other we got a children's book that we were trying to distribute, and it wasn't selling. I asked him why. I said, "What's the trouble? Why can't we get these children's books going?" And he explained that most of the evangelists he knew did not believe that children could come to Christ. They believed that people have to be adults before they can come to that point of decision.

So there was no burden for winning children among any of the evangelists, and these were good, strong, evangelical evangelists. These were not people that were liberal. It was just that the mindset of village India at that time believed that way. It is not the mindset today, thank God. But it was at that time. Evangelists believed that it was a waste of time to preach the Gospel to children, because they were too young to make any decision for Christ.

So we called these evangelists together for some training. This was one of the reasons we started the schools for evangelists, and one of the subjects Joyce taught was child evangelism.

Joyce: My first class had twenty-one men. One young man was just beginning in evangelism; the rest were quite experienced. I asked them how many had led even one child to the Lord. No hands went up. I stood in that classroom and I said, "Okay, let's just talk about this."

So at the end of that time that they were there, that four weeks, I challenged them to see how many children they could bring to the Lord during the next three months, because at that time they were in for training one month and out in the field three months. When they came back, I asked how many adults they had led to Christ, and it came to 262. And then I added up how many children had been won to Christ, and it was 259. Three souls difference. And they were ecstatic. They never knew this was possible before. That changed the whole atmosphere for child evangelism.

Bill: So when the men started to do evangelism among children, they were in seventh heaven almost, because the children were so responsive, and so many came to Christ. In a real sense this was a pioneer effort in rural India. In urban India there were some classes for children in the big churches that were western oriented, so there was CBS and some child evangelism in the big urban churches.

DB: CBS?

Bill: Children's Bible Schools. Something like what's called VBS, Vacation Bible Schools in America. This was completely new for rural India when we started those. And it revolutionized some of the evangelists. Some evangelists said, "I've led more people to Christ in the last three months than I have in all my life," because they were now reaching children. That's why IBL then aggressively moved into Children's Bible Schools.

One of our staff had funding for a couple of hundred children, from America. An individual was giving funding for him to reach a couple of hundred children, which he was doing, in a small way, through an organization in India. He shared that with us, and I thought, "That's good. We will take that up as an IBL ministry." We started it as an IBL ministry, and it just exploded, until today we're reaching about two million, and now we're stabilized at that. Two million children a year, and we want to move on from that. That's the present base from which we mean to expand.

Bill Teate: I have here the figures that I'm sharing with the churches. In 1990 the number was 3,000 children, and then the next year, it was 30,000, and then in 1992, it was 300,000. In 1993, it was 500,000. In 1994, it doubled to a million, and in

1995 it doubled again to 2 million.

And then what I'm always telling the pastors is that people were saying to Bill Scott, "Oh, next year, three million, four million." Do you know how many we did the next year? Back to a million and a half. Quality control, because Bill Scott saw there was waste, and he wanted to tighten up the program and not just grow for the sake of numbers."

Bill: That's very accurate. Bill knows the figures.

DB: And now it's stabilized at around two million?

Bill: Yes, two million. But that is just a base from which to start the next phase of growth.

# Chapter 19

# What If They Can't Read?

Joyce: One day in the fall of 1967 I got a call from our Baptist mission office headquarters. Ruth Thurman, who is now with the Lord, was our field secretary then, and she said, "Joyce, could I challenge you to take up the literacy work for our Telugu Baptist Churches?"

It was a new field for me, but I only had to think a few seconds before I said, "Okay, Ruth, I'll do it."

It's strange, because early on I had said that I never wanted to be a teacher, but every year after college, and then after language study in India, I was teaching in some way. But developing a literacy program was truly a challenge.

DB: What was the literacy rate in India at that time?

Joyce: About 27%. Close to three-quarters of the people of India could not read anything. At about the same time the Andhra Christian Council of Churches asked me to become chairman of their work in literacy in Andhra Pradesh state, and I was also asked to be on the literacy committee of the Council of Christian Churches for all of India. This gave me a national exposure to whatever was going on in the field of literacy training. So I learned a lot.

I started working on primers in Telugu, but the big push came after Bill and I felt led to move to the city of Madras in late 1975, after 25 years in the villages. It was a real battle, because the Lord really had to change my feeling about moving to the city.

Bill established the work in a little house. Later we shifted it to a slightly larger house, with room for our offices and inventory of Bibles. I was doing my Baptist mission work, but one day Bill said, "Joyce, would you be willing to come and join me in this work?" I prayed about it, and thought about it, and wondered really what I would do if I did eventually give up the mission assignments and work 100% with him. But the answer was yes. So eventually I gave up the mission assignments, and I came in to work with him as Associate General Director of India Bible Literature.

One day I sat and prayed, "Lord, why am I here? Tell me, what is it I am to do?" I saw little things daily that I could help with here or there, but I wanted the big picture.

The Lord spoke to me so clearly. "Joyce, there will come a day when Scriptures will not be allowed to be distributed in India. I want you to help flood India with My Word before that day comes." So I took on more responsibility.

Then came the question, "What about literacy?" The usefulness of distributing Bibles is limited if people can't read. You can only reach the people who can read what you are getting into their hands.

In 1976, Dr. Robert Rice, a missionary to Korea for fifteen years, had come home and started Literacy Evangelism International. He began to go to different countries to help them construct primers for literacy that had Bible content. Somebody who knew us in India met him, and Bob Rice asked him, "Do you know anybody in India working with literacy?" "Yes," he said, "Joyce Scott is working with literacy," and he gave Bob Rice my name and address.

Bob wrote to me, and then in the spring of 1976 he came to our house. I called in about nine or ten people. For two weeks we sat together in my home and wrote the primer set that we are now using in Telugu. There are three books in the set, plus the teacher's manual, and the whole thing is built on Bible content, saturated with Bible content. Now I had done a Telugu primer before. It had a couple of Bible stories in it, but it wasn't fully Bible, like that.

Just at that point we had to go on furlough, and very little happened until we got back. There were a few people here and a few people there who were asking for these primers, but the program wasn't set up as I would like to have had it set up.

We had asked Bibles for India if they would pay for the printing of these primers. They looked at me and said, "Well, can you prepare a rationale as to why there should be any literacy for our next board meeting?"

Well, that was a challenge. I wrote what I had to say because I couldn't get to the meeting.

Just about that time I wrote to a young couple who had written to us. Looking back, we do not know why, and they don't know why. But they had been doing a little literacy work up in our Baptist area. They had been working with World Vision, but had just recently left that work to go into something else. He was a college professor, and she could have been.

They responded, and came for an interview. I invited them to join us to help in teacher training, because people have to be trained how to teach adults. It's not like teaching children.

Among our first five projects were three among the Banjara gypsy tribes. In a year, the men who led those three projects dedicated three churches among the previously illiterate Banjara gypsies who had never heard the Gospel. They had gone to the classes to learn to read and write, but in doing that, as they studied those Bible-based primers, they were receiving the Word of God into their spirits. And, of course, we know that the Holy Spirit attends God's Word and bears witness to them that this is the truth. That was really the beginning.

In order to receive foreign funds for literacy, or any program in India as far as that goes, you need to be registered, and you also have to have a Foreign Contributions Regulatory Act approved bank account. We call it FCRA. The Lord spoke to me, and I kept hearing the name, Literacy India Trust. If we ever need to register with the government, this is what I want to call this, Literacy India Trust.

Then the Lord really impressed this direction on my spirit: "I want you to sit down, sit down and write this literacy program." Not primers, but just how this literacy program would operate. The methodology, perhaps, we could say.

So for about ten days every night after supper for a couple hours I would sit and write, and it just came rolling out. The Holy Spirit was just giving me every bit of this, from every angle, every approach, and how it should be run, requirements, all kinds of things.

In the end I had this manual, what was the working manual, and we're still using that same manual. I never knew while I was doing that for ten nights in a row, Don, that the Lord was bringing the whole program together, taking all that He had deposited within me and bringing that out into a concrete program that was going to go all over India, from north to south and from east to west. A few are even going into Burma and Nepal and Bhutan and Sikkim now. There is Bible knowledge going into those unreached and closed areas through literacy.

In 1987 the World Home Bible League was only willing to give us enough materials to sponsor 6,000 students a year. I said to Bill, "You know, I just feel so strongly like I'm being bound. And more and more people are coming."

Now, Don, when we look back to 1967 when I started to do literacy work with the Baptist Mission, we could hardly get anybody's ear or even a second look. But when we started this program, in 1984 and 1985 and 1986, people who wanted this began to come out of the woodwork. The more success they heard about, the more people have come and applied, wanting to run a literacy project, and they come to ask us to fund it.

We do make them apply. We have a form the applicant has to fill out. We need to know what his qualifications are. Does he know the Lord? We have to have his personal testimony, his church affiliations, and who will be involved with the literacy training program. We even ask for his picture.

DB: You mentioned a "project." How big is a project?

Bill: Five villages. Five classes.

Joyce: Five classes with thirty in a class, 150 people.

DB: That's one project?

Joyce: That's one project and one person. Maybe he's an

evangelist out there, a pastor, a teacher, or just a Christian businessman, and he's concerned. He'll come and apply.

If we approve his application, he comes for what we call "Project Officer Orientation Seminar." He goes through that, gets all the information, goes through the manual that I wrote, and learns what we expect. Then we interview him.

Now if we find some caginess about him, any deceit, something not quite right, that makes us feel he's not being fully honest, we say, "Thank you, we'll let you know."

But suppose we say, "This fellow's genuine. He really loves the Lord, he's got a vision, and he has a burden." Then we put down, "Approved." Then we write and tell him, "You bring your teachers, your five teachers, to be trained."

Then he has to spend another six days with us. He's already had five or six with us now. When we set the various locations for the training we're going to do in the various languages—like Telugu, Tamil, Hindi—he has to come with his five teachers. If he does not come, he doesn't get his project. Because how does he know what to expect from his teachers he will be supervising if he himself is not trained in teaching? So the Project Officer gets the training, too. If he doesn't come, his name is just crossed off.

It costs us $20 for each student to have them go through the course for ten months, to learn to read and write.

DB: Twenty dollars for a ten-month course? Is that all?

Joyce: Right. Twenty dollars for one student to study ten months to learn to read and write. Plus each sponsoring organization contributes six dollars per learner, over and above that twenty, toward costs.

DB: The organization pays only $6 per student for the ten-month course? Is that a lot of money for the village people?

Bill: It is. Quite a lot.

DB: So this is another partnership situation, where churches, Christians around the world can help?

**Bill & Joyce:** Yes, that's right!

DB: And the result is that you train one adult to read?

Joyce: One adult illiterate who becomes a neoliterate.

Bill: Five nights a week, two hours a night, ten months.

DB: That's quite a commitment.

Bill & Joyce: Yes, it is.

DB: And they are paying what is a substantial amount for them?

Joyce: They are paying for consumable goods: for chalk, because they're using a good bit of it, and for kerosene, which is very expensive, for the kerosene lights.

Bill: So it's a big commitment, commitment of time as well as commitment of money.

Joyce: Yes, and the organization has to pay...

Bill: ...This is where the partnership comes in.

Joyce: The organization has to pay for all the registration costs and materials, like attendance books and progress report books. They also pay for any special extras for people coming in — extras like making them aware of health needs, or giving them some awareness about kitchen gardening or raising goats or small-time dairy, all the different ways we're trying to make them aware of what they can do for themselves.

Now, I am five hundred percent in favor of getting people to do what they can do for themselves. That was the whole idea when I was back at the school in Peddapalli, doing this basic education, teaching them how to do crafts — carpentry and tailoring and other things — because they need to have something that is productive, that they can work with their own hands.

And so, when we bring these applicants in to run a project, we want people who care about a lot more than just getting the illiterates to the place where they can say, "Well, now he can read and write, or she can read and write." That is important! We know that. Just reading and writing is important. Now a woman can sign her name instead of using a thumbprint. She can actually pick up a pen and write her name. She can read the bus names, where the destinations of the buses are. She can tell whether she's going into the ladies' toilet or the men's toilet. She can read a bottle of medicine — "This is poison; don't do this, and don't do that"—instead of not being able to read it, taking it, and dying because she couldn't read the instructions.

These are very basic things we don't even think about. But this literacy program is not just for the head. She can read the Bible, but it's more than that. Because as they are learning to read and write all these different little curlicues called letters, they are also having the Word of God deposited in their hearts.

In the meantime they've learned a lot of practical, everyday living things. They've learned the vocabulary they need for shopping in the bazaar, for work, and everything else they have to do. They've got that. So you can see that what I wanted was much more, and why we insist on Project Officers who want much more.

What I wanted comes out of what I was thinking about way back when I considered whether to take up the literacy program with our Baptist church. I took a survey then, and I found out that of our 230,000 Baptist believers in that small part of India, only 16.4% of the women and only about 18% of the men could read and write. That virtually gives you a church without a Bible.

Bill: An illiterate church.

Joyce: An illiterate church. Many of the young pastors, these fellows who were coming out as evangelists and pastors, weren't much beyond that. So I'm thinking, "Okay, how are we going to equip them?" That's the word I want to use. Bill used it when he was talking about equipping the evangelists.

We started through literacy to equip the church with readers. That was my burden, to bring these precious people who had heard, who had responded, but who did not know how to pick up the book or which way to hold it, let alone how to read God's love letter.

So our motto is "Equip the church to grow in Christ."

DB: Do you have an age limit policy about who can enroll to study in these classes?

Joyce: The government takes students between the ages of 15 and 35. They won't take anybody over 35. We start teaching children from the age of 13, and we go right on up to…well, the oldest person we have ever taught was a dear 85-year-old woman. Can you imagine at 85? But her motivation was, "I must read the Word of God."

So we had literacy projects in 15 states out of the 26 in India in 1998. We had to cancel some because we really monitor carefully to maintain quality. We started out with 56,520 learners, but we ended up 1998 with 53,370.

Every person who completes the course gets a Bible in the literacy festival at the end, not just a certificate. Many people are really studying hard through the ten months, so that they can get a Bible free. That's the one thing they get free. But they've paid for it in sacrifice and dedication after ten months!

Now to show how it has grown, in 1984 we only had five centers, with a total of 150 students. We had 80% success. Then in 1985, still in just one state, we had five projects, 31 centers, 930 students, and still 80%. So it goes on, growing year by year. The total number of learners who have gone through this ten-month program now comes to 368,520. And the success rate has kept growing. Of all of those who start the course, men and women, 88% complete it successfully on average. One year it was 91%.

DB: They learn to read while learning about Jesus. Do you have any figures on how many then become Christians?

Joyce: It varies depending on where they are from. But I have 42% as an average. Often there are more from the south than from the north. From the north we may get some 35–37%.

Bill: The overall average over the years is 42%.

DB: That would mean about 150,000 new believers out of this literacy program! And I'm sure a group of new churches?

Joyce: Oh, yes! Churches are being born. The Bible content is the thing that the Holy Spirit uses to bring these people to Christ. We have three books in the series, and in lesson ten of the first book they hear the name Jesus. From there on, as they learn different letters, as soon as we can begin to tell the story of Jesus, we tell it. They begin to learn that there is a man by that name, and who He was, and what He did. By the end of the three primers, it's all there: His birth, His life, His ministry, His death, His resurrection, the purpose of His coming, and so on. In the last of the three there are twenty-six stories about Jesus. It's all there, along with all the other material that has to do with their own nation and people and life in the village.

We reach all kinds of people through these literacy classes, people of different castes, different tribes, and even different religions. The impact is dramatic in all of these situations. We get reports on the number of prayer cells that are formed from these literacy centers, and virtually all of them become churches.

DB: So when thirty people go through a ten-month course, some ten or fifteen—twelve on the average—become believers, and start a prayer cell that eventually becomes a church?

Bill: That's right.

Joyce: In some places, 100% of the people come to Christ.

DB: Since you ended up with 53,370 learners last year, that would be about 1,800 literacy centers and 1,800 new churches?

Bill: That's right.

Joyce: Yes. To be precise, there were 1,884 centers last year. That's 1,884 new churches.

Bill Teate: There's another fringe benefit of the literacy program, Joyce, that you have told us about—the teachers.

Joyce: There are times where we can't get enough Christian teachers. We try for all Christian teachers in the villages. In a project, where we're going to have five classes, we like to have five Christian teachers.

But there are places where there is maybe just one Christian teacher, or none. Still, there's a village evangelist or pastor there who wants to introduce the Jesus-based literacy classes. Then, he has to use Hindu teachers who are willing to teach it, even though they are going to be teaching about Jesus. Invariably, they all come to Christ! Because they are teaching the Word of God through these three primers, you see.

There's one fellow who deliberately uses Hindu teachers.

This last time I interviewed him, I asked, "Why do you have two Christians and three Hindus?" "Well," he said, "you approved that last year." I said, "You had it last year, but now you're doing it again. Don't you have some other Christians?" He said, "That's one of my modes of evangelism. Hindu teachers are coming to Christ. So if I take two or three, you know, they're going to come to Christ. That's evangelism." What could I say?

DB: Let me ask you a couple of questions to help put all this in perspective. What is the overall literacy of India today?

Joyce: About thirty percent.

DB: So illiteracy is seventy percent. Does the government hold classes or organize programs to teach people how to read?

Joyce: They have what they call the National Literacy Mission, which everybody got excited about in the early 1990s. But what they have actually accomplished has been disappointing. Some claim that they have been ten percent successful, but figures like that are often padded.

DB: And you have an average 88 percent success rate?

Joyce: That's right.

DB: And in addition to learning to read in your programs, they learn the Scripture. They learn the story of Jesus.

Joyce: They do. But I should emphasize that we also have a broad spectrum of what we call content sheets or awareness sheets. These give them teaching about their physical needs. They teach how to take care of their eyes, what to do about common illnesses, how to keep the rats out of their homes and out of their grain, the importance of pure drinking water, practical things like that for their daily life. Bill also put in a simple accounting system they can use in their homes, or in their cottage industry, so that they can learn to keep accounts.

We also include information about prenatal and postnatal care for mothers. There is also a section on the various government programs they can use, programs dealing with savings, banking, agriculture, small animal husbandry, and things like that.

## What If They Can't Read?

DB: The literacy training also makes it easier for the women to earn money for their families, doesn't it?

Joyce: Oh, yes. That's one of the most obvious results.

DB: So you've contributed to the spiritual life, to the economic life, to the social life, their ability to participate in the political life of the country—you touch about everything!

Joyce: Oh, yes. We get piles of reports of human interest stories, and for every story we hear there are hundreds we don't hear.

We heard of one woman, for example, who was a very harsh person. She argued with everybody in the village, she swore, and she had a very difficult relationship with her husband. After she went to the literacy program and had some success, she began to have personal respect for herself. She made a complete turn around. She started to get along with her husband. She stopped her swearing and her chewing and all the rest of it.

DB: Chewing? What do you mean by chewing?

Joyce: They have a nut called the betel nut. It's not tobacco, but they use it something like tobacco. It's a sort of drug. And she stopped that, and stopped arguing with all the neighbors and people in the village, so her whole life was changed. The societal changes alone are very significant.

I was talking recently to one of our project officers working with our literacy program among the Santali tribes. There are about ten million people in the Santali tribes. They are a tribe that the government is not doing too much with. Consequently they are very far behind many other areas of India, economically, educationally, and even socially.

The Santali primers were written just a couple of years ago, with the help of the same Dr. Robert Rice I mentioned before. His work is based in Tulsa, Oklahoma. When that was finished, we printed the primers. The Catholics came and asked us for ten thousand. We printed only ten thousand sets; there are three books in that series, and they wanted the whole ten thousand sets.

We went and trained the priests and the nuns how to use them, how to teach adults to read. We went through a six-day training course with them. They hadn't seen any literacy training methods like these before. Then our teacher-training staff went back into the Santali tribe with them, and they led them into the first Christmas celebration that they've ever had.

The Santali live way out, about fifty miles from the nearest rail station or bus line. So our people had gone out there just in rickety trucks and cars to get to where this training was taking place. The Santali people themselves really appreciated the fact that somebody cared enough to come all that distance, way back in the boondocks, in the mountains up there in the state of Bihar, to help them. They were impressed that anybody cared enough about them to be willing to go back into the tribal areas and to take the time to teach them how to read and write.

The thing that might surprise people outside of India is that people are really being changed, by the millions. I don't believe there is one single woman who has finished the ten-month course who hasn't had a major, positive, qualitative change, in her life.

One particular village woman comes to mind. It's the 85-year-old woman I mentioned earlier. She was in the Santali area, but closer to Calcutta. This woman got into the classes to learn to read. Now some would say, "Poor thing! Why would she struggle for ten months, at 85 years of age?" Even Indians asked that question. Some of them said, "Good night, why do you want to learn to read? You're 85; what difference does it make? You're close to the grave—forget about it!"

Well, this woman had tuberculosis of the spine. Surgery was done, but it had left her crippled so that she could not stand or walk. Every morning her family would pick her up and carry her out to a rope bed, nothing fancy, just a piece of cloth on top of the ropes, and put her there on the little front veranda of a mud hut. All day she was in that position. They held the class right there, with the other Santali women gathered around her, so that she could participate.

## What If They Can't Read?

She was asked, "Why are you learning to read?" She said, "All my life I've had to depend on somebody else to come read the Word of God to me. But I could never pick up the Bible for myself. Now I have determined that I want to learn to read God's Word so that I no longer have to depend on someone else and so that I can read it to others."

Today she is quite a testimony there. She calls out to all the women that pass her house, and many pass her house daily. She says, "Do you know how to read and write? You don't know how to read and write? You've got to come to this class, you've got to come and learn. You are blind; you're in a cave. You must come and have the light come into your mind."

She is a testimony for the Lord. She witnesses to them about the Lord. She calls people over and prays with them there, and it's just a real lighthouse in the middle of that Santali tribal area, back in the jungles and the forests. She is a blessing to many people. And it wasn't long before she was able to read the New Testament to other women there.

Another story happened in another village in the Santali tribal area, not far away. There was a literacy class set up to meet five nights a week, two hours every night, but they couldn't find a place to study. The women who live there didn't know where they could have it. So they said, "Okay, we'll go into that stable."

Now, personally, I would not like to go and sit for a couple of hours in a smelly stable. But these women went into that stable, and they pushed all the cattle over to the one side. Then they put down their grass mats on top of where all the animals had been during the day, and they held their class for a couple of hours that night. When they were finished, they rolled up their grass mats, took their lantern, put all the cows back in place again, and went home.

For ten months they did that. Such determination! "Nothing's going to stop us. Even if we don't have a place to meet, we're going to find a place, make a place, so that we can meet together and learn how to read and write."

There is another story from that same tribal atmosphere, along the border of Orissa and Andhra Pradesh. A number of our literacy classes are being held up there, being implemented by the ministry of a man called Swaminaden. His sons also help him in this, particularly one son by the name of Enoch.

Enoch told me that one day there was a knock at their door. And Enoch's specialty is the Telugu language. The Oriya language is spoken across the border of the state. There was a knock at the door, he went out, and there were two young fellows there. He said, "Yes, what can I do for you?"

They said, "We hear that you have literacy classes."

He answered, "Yes, we do. Where are you from?"

"Oh," they said, "we live over in Orissa state. We speak Oriya. But we don't have any literacy classes over there. We want to learn to read and write."

Enoch said, "But this is Telugu."

They said, "Wee speak Telugu, because we're on the border. We speak both. But it doesn't make any difference. We will come every day." It was about twelve miles of travel. "We will come every day in the evening and go back at night. We are willing to walk the twelve miles every day and come to learn, even in another language, so that we can at least read and write Telugu, since we can't have the classes in our own language."

Over the course of the ten months, they walked 4,800 miles. That's motivation. It really confirms what we have found out, and what we know in our hearts about these people. There is a great hunger to be able to read and write, especially among Christians who cannot read and write, so that they can read the Word of God.

I remember a story Bill was referring to about a time in our Baptist mission where we were talking to a group of women about starting a literacy class. A 75-year-old woman stood up and said, "I want a class here."

I said, "You're an elderly woman; why do you want this?"

She bowed her head down and said, "Well, I know I'm not long for this world. I don't have too many years left to live here," she said, "but I've never been able to read God's Word, and I do not want to die and go to heaven and face my Lord, embarrassed, that I have never been able to open the Book and read His letter to me."

This is hard for many of us to take in. We have no idea of what it is like to feel that way, because among the first things we can remember, we recall Mommy and Daddy holding books in front of us and reading to us. Then we read for ourselves and in school. But to the illiterate, the funny little curlicues we call letters mean nothing until we teach them.

DB: Joyce, you said that you keep control over these, and you cancel some. Is your reason they have to send reports to make sure that they're using the money right, so people who are partners from this end can be sure that this money is effectively used?

Joyce: That's right. We do it for that reason; but we do it also for effectiveness—to keep the program a success. People are beginning to learn that if they do not do things right, if they do not meet the requirements that we have, month by month, then they do not get their next month's money for their teachers. We pay the teachers 200 rupees a month for their teaching. That's a nice small stipend. But the teachers are not going to get that if the project officer who is their supervisor doesn't do what he's supposed to do.

DB: What kinds of things do you check?

Joyce: Primarily we check what they are doing with the money, and we check whether they're teaching with our methods or whether they've taken to some government thing that does not have any Christianity in it. We get pretty complete reports, and we have it all on computer. Every project is on the computer.

We also get case histories of what happens in the lives of many of the people involved. What we're really interested in, of course, is seeing who's being changed, lives changed, lives transformed as people turn to Jesus—seeing the impact of the literacy programs for the Gospel.

This is one of the things that has been the biggest thrill to me, because we want to equip the church to grow in Christ. The first time it happened was when a man named Kamalakar, who works with the Yanadi peoples, came to me and said, "Guess what!" I said, "What's going on?" He said, "One of my neo-literates [a new reader] came to me and said he has found Christ during these ten months, and he thinks Christ is calling him to be an evangelist. So, what can I do?" Now Kamalakar had an SOE running, so he told the man, "Okay, we'll enter you into the School of Evangelism."

Now that man, ten months earlier, hadn't a clue about reading and writing. He didn't have a Bible, he couldn't read it, he had no songbooks, or anything. Ten months later, he's reading, he has come to Christ, he feels a call of God on his life, and he goes and trains for another year in the School of Evangelism. It's people like him who make the best evangelists, according to all the reports we get.

I remember a story about a small congregation up among the tribal villages in the north, near Nellore. The pastor one day invited people to ask for prayer. One sickly lady came up, and he thought she was going to ask for healing. But she said she wanted to hold a Bible in her hand and read it. He was really surprised, but she got into one of our literacy classes, and started going to his church.

She was a very inquisitive sort of person, and very anxious to learn everything she could about Jesus. Now there's a Bible verse on every lesson in the literacy classes, and they're supposed to learn it. And one of the verses she had learned was John 1: 1, *"In the beginning was the Word, and the Word was with God, and the Word was God."*

One day as she was going to the worship service, a young Hindu man saw her, and he knew that she was an illiterate. Seeing a Bible under her arm, he went up to her and decided to make fun of her. He asked her, sarcastically, what she was holding in her hand.

She said, "I'm holding God." He thought that was a great

joke, but he was sort of stunned to hear her answer that way. He just sort of stared at her, and then after taking a long breath he asked her what she meant by saying she was holding God. Looking intently at this fellow, she explained that she was attending a literacy class, and that she had learned from John 1:1 that the Word was God.

The young man was so surprised to hear this response that he followed her to church the next Sunday, and the Sunday after that. After attending for three weeks, he accepted Jesus as his Savior. Today, that young man has become very zealous for the Lord, to serve him in any way that he can.

There's another story I think is just miraculous. In a village called Tharigoppula, also in Andhra state, a literacy class was started among beggar boys. Now these boys spent all their time begging or stealing. It was a community thing. Everybody was like this in that village, not just the boys. They grew up in beggar families.

The literacy class started, and about twelve of these boys in their early teens came to learn to read and write. The classes were in the evening. By the time they finished the course, ten months later, every one of them had accepted Christ. They went back to their families and said, "Listen, it's not right to live by begging. The Bible says that we must earn our own living." "Oh," said their families, "that's just that Christianity they're forcing down your throats." But the boys kept talking with their families, and the families listened. "No, no," they would say, "you think about it. This is really wrong. You're taking from people. We've not earned it."

And this is the miracle. Before long, the ideas that had been planted in those boys seeped into the families and seeped all through that community. It was completely changed. Finally it got to the point where the village council said, "Anybody who begs will be boycotted."

There was a stone idol that was at the entrance to the village, but people began to come to Christ. More and more of them left that stone idol, and they began to meet under a tree.

Before long they started looking at their houses. They were tiny little things, maybe four feet long, or three feet, made of bent pieces of bamboo, pieces of plastic, old pieces of broken grass matting, made of any old scraps. They lived in those, along with their pigs. And those twelve boys started saying, "Well, we're not going to live like this. Why should we accept this way of our fathers and mothers? This isn't the way to live."

They went to the government and applied for housing grants, and because they were neo-literates, people who had just learned to read, the government said, "Okay." So each family went and applied for money to build a new house, a good house, of brick and cement. Not big ones, but brick and cement with tile roofing. I have a picture of a house that's almost completed, and in front of it is one of these little tiny mud-and-bamboo things. That certainly shows the difference between what was before these boys learned to read and became Christian.

Then those who had accepted Christ, the ones who had been baptized, started putting money together. On the other side of that little stone temple, there's a beautiful little church, cement and brick and tile roofing. The stone idol is no longer worshipped, because now everybody in that village became Christian. Everybody. Everybody was baptized. Nobody was begging. All because twelve boys learned how to read and write with materials based on the life of Jesus. So, along with reading and writing skills, they found the value of life, the ethics of life, the whole change that happens with God, and their lives were different.

DB: And they spread it!

Joyce: And they spread it.

Bill: Praise the Lord. Actually, in India, there's a man of God who feels—and I agree with him—that the greatest social service agent in the world is the Gospel of Jesus Christ. He says that through the Gospel and all it brings with it, including literacy, there is more effective social uplift than through any other kind of program.

In other words, he says that when churches pay for other kinds of social uplift programs, that is going about things the wrong way. The best way to achieve social uplift is to get people redeemed, and then the whole community is uplifted socially. Did I tell about the village that was transformed and became productive through beekeeping?

DB: No.

Bill: Well, that's one very fine example of this. An engineer was called by God, sent by God, to go up into a jungle area of beggars and thieves, one like we have been describing, a place where people did not work, and everything they got was through stealing and through deceit. It was just beggars and thieves. He went up into that area as a Gospel preacher.

It was one of the most depraved areas in the state and in the nation of India. He went up there and brought the Gospel of Jesus Christ. One family was redeemed, and another, until after a few years there was a church there.

But after a few years something else happened, like what Joyce shared now. The beggars now said, "It is wrong to beg." The thieves now said, "It is wrong to steal. We must work, and if we do not work, we are not true Christians." That's the way they read the Bible. They take it very seriously and very plainly. It says if you are a Christian, you should work and earn what you get. So they all started to work.

This engineer-evangelist introduced the idea of producing honey through the raising of bees. That community became a model community. They built beautiful homes, clean homes. The children became educated, going to school. The families were working, and they had beautiful gardens, flowers and vegetables outside.

There was such a transformation in that community that it was recognized by the government of India as one of the most significant socioeconomic developed areas in the whole of the state, and a model for the nation of India. The government officials asked, "What social action program caused this to happen? How was it changed from what it was to what it is now?"

This man said, "The Gospel of Jesus Christ."

When we hear stories like this, we're talking about the hope of a nation, and we're seeing it happen. That's what makes me excited as we see this happening.

When we see a thousand new churches, it's not only that. It's a thousand beacons. We're talking about a power that changes an individual, and then it changes a family, and when it's released it changes a community, which can ultimately change the nation. The new churches are places that are going to affect entire communities, then the state, and the nation. It's a transformation, a socioeconomic developmental transformation that is second to none.

So if you want to get involved in social work, the Gospel is the best way to do it. And when communities are changed, others want to know how it happened, and the Gospel spreads.

*Joyce:* We have so many, so many stories like this. We get at least two stories every month from every literacy project. The project officer will tell us about people in his project whose lives are changed. The girl that I have working in my office has gone over 15,962 case histories like that. That's a small percentage of the over 350,000 people who have gone through the literacy training in the first five or six years, but many more have been reached. Still, this will give you an idea about the kind of thing that happens.

We receive stories about the different kinds of things that happen in their lives when they learn to read and have accepted Christ. They may start a little business, a little shop in the village, they may take up tailoring, or carpentry, you know, something to improve themselves.

In some places economic co-ops are started, savings and loans. In some places nobody ever heard about saving, never thought about it. But after the literacy programs got in, everybody began to save. Then the church improved the wells, stopped liquor, all these kind of things are in the reports that we get, more than you could have time to read.

We have found that this is an entrance. Leaders of literacy

projects can get into villages where there has been a definite strong Hindu rejection of Christianity. The literacy classes are what open up the doors to the Gospel, again and again.

DB: You know, it strikes me as ironic that the American and British churches where everybody knows how to read are really no better off than a church in India. Over there, only 18% can read the Bible; here I would guess that only 18% do read the Bible. Many of our churches are illiterate about God, by their own choice.

Bill: That's an interesting thought.

DB: I would guess that there's going to be more vitality in the Indian church, where everybody who can read does read, than in our churches where people can read but spend their time reading almost anything but the Bible.

Bill: I think that's true.

Joyce: This reminds me of a story about a Christian doctor up in Andhra Pradesh. She was feeling that she wanted to get into an area where there was very little medical service. She and her husband went there, set up a clinic, and began to try to minister to these people, as Christians in the medical field. But they were having very little response.

She applied to us because the place was almost totally illiterate. It was very, very low in literacy percentage, very few people reading. She applied to us. We gave her a project. Remember that one project is five villages. As those classes got under way, slowly, after three or four months, people began to come to them. They came for their medical services, and they began also to hear the Gospel.

Then the people who were studying, the adults, the parents, pleaded with her to start a school for their children. They did not want to perpetuate their illiteracy with their children. So she and her husband started a small school, a primary school. Then it went to an elementary school. Then it went to a middle school. Then it went to a high school. Now she has a junior college there, and several churches have been built. Also they are now able to minister through their medical work.

When she wrote about this, she said it was all because the literacy project opened the doors that regular missions could not break down.

So we praise God for all that happens. We hope to have a Bible in the hands of every single Indian family within a very few years, possibly less than three years. The literacy programs, the way we have been able to set them up with such a high success rate and with the teaching about Jesus, has the potential for making a strong and clear impact on the whole nation of India. The continuing growth of this literacy ministry is one of our highest priorities.

Bill: You need to ask Joyce about the new literacy course and the new literacy program, the Village Literacy Rehabilitation Projects.

# The Scott Ministry Album

## Literature and Bible Distribution

**Some of the literature that is distributed by IBL in Madras**

**Staff members counting and packing among the stacks of stored materials at IBL**

# The Scott Ministry Album

## Literature and Bible Distribution

**Packages being taken in a cycle cart to the rail station to be shipped off**

**CBS materials from IBL being carried away by the CBS leaders to be used in CBS classes**

**Little children taking "Guide to Happiness" book-lets home**

# The Scott Ministry Album

## Children's Bible School

**Children singing a song at CBS**

**Children's play at CBS**

## Children's Bible School

**Children presenting a play at a CBS closing function**

**CBS — 1999**

# The Scott Ministry Album

## Literacy Programs

**Teacher training in the literacy program**

**A teacher shows on a roll blackboard how to draw letters.**

# The Scott Ministry Album

## Literacy Programs

An elderly gentleman demonstrates his knowledge of letters and words in a lettering class.

Pastor M. G. Kisku giving the inaugural speech for the literacy program. New students received lanterns, primers, blackboards, and slates. Graduating students were given Bibles.

Joyce assists in an urban church as Bibles are being distributed to people who successfully completed the literacy classes.

# Chapter 20

# Village Literacy Rehabilitation Projects

**D**B: Village Literacy Rehabilitation Projects? Joyce, what's this?

**Bill Teate:** It's wonderful!

**Joyce:** Yes, it really is. We started out in 1984 with the ten-month literacy projects. In 1994 we had a ten-year festival for all the Project Officers with whom we had worked over that ten-year period. Sixteen hundred people came, teachers and project officers.

At that time, John DeVries was visiting in India, and Bill arranged his tour so that he could visit that conference. He was amazed, dumbfounded, absolutely shocked to see the extent of the literacy program and its impact at that time. He began to get interested in developing that as one of the ministries they would help to fund, and he took the opportunity to speak to some of my area coordinators and project officers to collect some good stories he could use to encourage churches to give.

Meanwhile, we were thinking about it and how we could improve it. Our board in India considered various ideas that came from America, but in the end they decided to act instead on some ideas we developed with them in India.

My program coordinator there had a doctorate in adult education. We had a lot of discussion about what we could do, and the goal we came up with was to take a village of about 250 homes, where we would find on average about 1,500 illiterates, and plan to bring them all to literacy within four years.

The impact would include the founding of a new church

and the economic and social transformation of the village. Since each class is about thirty people, that would mean that we would need fifty classes, about thirteen classes a year for four years. We also added new objectives that would make each class more intensive and far reaching than our ten-month classes. We wanted to make sure that the whole village would be changed, not just the individuals.

Bill: Would you say that the focus on this, as compared with your regular literacy work, was that you change a person and a family in regular literacy work, while this was now changing a whole community? Uplifting the community?

Joyce: Yes, the whole village.

Bill: So you were moving now from the individual family focus to the total community focus; would that be right?

Joyce: Exactly. And the interesting thing about this is that the government has talked about pushing literacy ever since independence. India has had five-year plans ever since 1948.

Bill: Ever since we've been married.

Joyce: Yes, five-year development plans, one after the other, just like in Russia. Literacy is always in each plan, but it has never gotten results, or even high priority. About ten years ago they started again with a National Literacy Mission, trying to put it in all the states, but it has been disappointing.

The beautiful thing is that government men have come to me and said, "Why is it that your program is such a success, and ours are doing little or nothing?" I just said, very plainly, "Because we have the dynamic of Christ in our lives and in our work and in the program." They can't say anything, because they see it working.

We talked with Dr. Malcolm Adi Sheshayya. He was in the UN, working in UNESCO, I believe, and he became a very prominent man. He was particularly interested and burdened for literacy. He came from a Catholic background, married a Hindu woman, but his interest was strictly secular. I got to know him, and I brought him to conferences and training sessions that we had.

When he saw what was happening in our literacy program and the changes in people, he could hardly believe it. Even then he could not believe that any adult could learn to read the Tamil Bible or the Telugu Bible within ten months. Now he is known and respected all over the world. So I thought, "All right, I'll show him."

So the next time we invited him, I also asked for a man and a woman from our literacy programs to come. Both of them were over 50 years old, and from about 75 miles away. Dr. Sheshayya was sitting beside me, and I had them come up one at a time. He knew the Bible, so I said, "You ask them what to read." He gave them a reference. They found it; they read it. He was astounded. He gave them more, and they kept finding and reading them. He got up and said to the crowd, "Mrs. Scott has proved me wrong." Well, I was a little embarrassed, since he is one of the most renowned men in literacy and adult education around the world. So I said, "No, I haven't proved him wrong. I've just proved that we're right."

DB: But the government has not started to use your Jesus-centered literacy materials to teach literacy, have they?

Joyce: No. They have sometimes said they are having success with their own programs. They have even declared one or two states completely literate, but few believe those claims.

Now with this new approach, we were determined to bring about real, fundamental change in an entire village within less than their five-year time frame. We put together a structure, an outline, and explained what we were going to do, and got some enthusiastic response. A lot of people applied to lead the first of these whole village projects, but we carefully selected a few of our veteran teachers who had done much more in the ten-month program than just teach literacy.

You know, Don, we have never wanted to teach literacy just to enable people to say, "Okay, I can read this, 'The cat went up the tree.'" That would only make it possible for them to read communist literature, anti-social literature, and so on.

As you know, our primary goal was getting the Word of

God into their hearts. For that reason we always encouraged all our literacy teachers to think about spirit, soul, and body in their approach to their students. So we looked at a number of our veterans who had already been doing extra things with their people.

We chose five to begin with, and we called them in. We told them all our plans for Village Literacy Rehabilitation Projects, and asked, "Are you interested?" Every last one of them snapped it up.

We worked with them to find and identify a village where we would find 250 homes with approximately 1500 illiterates. So we began to give them the money to start the pilot programs.

DB: What does the money go for?

Joyce: First, some goes to the teachers. They get 200 rupees a month for a year, since this program runs for a year, not ten months. Then we pay for a blackboard, slates for the students, three primers for each student,

Bill: Lights,…

Joyce: Yes, lights, something like a Coleman lantern. You need those, since the classes are at night.

Bill: And you should know that the 200 rupees a month is not a living wage. It's just a stipend.

Joyce: That's right. The teachers must support themselves. They are people who have jobs. They may be clerks, teachers, or they may be living with their family and getting help that way. They could be college students, or even older high school students.

DB: What is a living wage?

Bill: In a village? About 800 rupees, so we're giving them about a quarter of a normal living wage for teaching five nights a week.

Joyce: One of the first men who said yes was Solomon Bijja. He is a very fine Christian man, working way down in the jungles of a southern state, Tamilnadu. He has been working in isolated areas among the people who are Afro-Indians. Back in colonial days, the British imported some Africans as servants, and they settled there. There was some intermarriage, and these Afro-Indians are a very neglected group. Groups like this are called "tribes" in India. The government doesn't seem interested in helping them much, either economically or educationally. Well, Solomon decided he was going to work among these Afro-Indian people.

When he first went in, they were very suspicious, but he kept loving them, caring for them, helping them meet some of their needs, and they began to trust him. Then he started talking about literacy. "Ha! Whoever heard of learning to read and write? Why bother?" There were no schools there at all.

He could have just said, "Well, I'm going to choose another area," but he kept at it. The first year he came back to talk with us, he had hardly anything good to say. He just told us what I'm telling you now. It was discouraging. The second year he came back, things were changing. They were beginning to open up, coming to classes, and taking his advice. In fact, a few of them had even decided to take his advice and start raising teak trees to help their economic situation. When the trees are ready to sell, they really bring in the money.

The third year he came back, we couldn't stop him talking. He was saying, "People are coming to Christ; people are being baptized; there are five prayer cells that have been formed out of the thirteen literacy classes. Everything's happening!"

He really got them going and motivated. They went to the government and asked for hardtop roads, and the government put one in. They asked for lights for the village; the government gave them. They asked for a bus stop, and the bus now is stopping there. They have to walk about a mile and a half to get to that bus, but before, there were no buses available whatsoever. They had to walk out in all the mud during the monsoons, and walk for miles and miles to get to any kind of a transport facility whatsoever.

Also, they started a little school for the children of these adults who had been illiterate people. Some of the parents are taking training in tailoring, some are starting little kitchen gardens. All kinds of good things are happening to that previously totally neglected area. Solomon now has even come asking for another project. Bill, what was that project he was doing, that you gave him the financing for getting started?

Bill: There was a teak wood project: when the teak trees start to mature, then of course they keep planting as they harvest, so they have a continual income, and it's a very high income product once it starts producing. And the second project, ... I can't remember exactly what it was.

Joyce: Anyway, Solomon is typical of what really happens in a new program. I receive all kinds of good reports, and it absolutely thrills us to see the changes, especially in areas like Solomon's that were just totally dead, and they're coming alive.

We call men like Solomon a Village Literacy Officer, because they are dealing with a whole village. The original ten-month literacy projects were to teach five classes of thirty students each in five different villages, 150 students, and the man in charge was a Project Officer. The new program is roughly ten times as large in scale, and the person in charge is called a Village Literacy Officer.

Now another Village Literacy Officer's name is John, and he is a very dynamic fellow. When he began to be an evangelist, he slept on railroad station platforms. He had no place to go.

Bill: That was because he came from a Hindu family. His name is John Selvaraj, and he wanted to work for God. But when he became a Christian, his family disinherited him, so he had no home. He just slept on the railway platform; that was his home. Everything he owned was in the little sack, a little bag that he had.

He lived on the goodwill of a few Christians, about ten or eleven believers that would give him some food. Somebody would give him food, and whatever he got that day, that's what he got. But now he has one of the biggest churches in the area, and he's got dozens of daughter churches and a mission outreach, and a lot of the growth has come about because of the literacy programs.

This is in one of the hardest areas in the state of Tamilnadu. Very hard, militant Hindus are very active there. But the church is growing there, dynamically. The more persecution, it seems, the greater the growth of the church.

Joyce: By the way, he first heard about India Bible Literature while he was sleeping on the railway station platform. He came on the train into Madras, found our IBL office, and talked to Bill about his ministry. He had never been to Bible school, and he went through one of our School of Evangelism programs. He was one of the first to go through the program in Madras before we started on-site schools in the villages.

Bill: Just to interject, he was an educated man. He was a college graduate, but had never gone to Bible school.

Joyce: So he got his Bible training then in that one year and went out, and believers began to come. He said, "I never knew what it was before to have goals." In the Schools of Evangelism they are taught about how to have goals, along with all the other things that they were learning. After a couple of years, he came and asked if he could have a literacy program, the basic ten-month program. He had a big success with that and applied again the following year. He did it for a number of years, repeated it year after year.

All the Project Officers must put in fresh applications, and we look at what they've done the previous year. He was doing a good job, going beyond just teaching them how to read and write. So we offered him one of the first Village Literacy Rehabilitation Projects, and he was thrilled with it. Prayer cells were coming out of literacy classes and becoming churches. So he had all these little daughter churches.

As his target for a Village Literacy Rehabilitation Project, he chose the village of Molasur, to make it a model village, 100% literate. He started with the help of some people who had come to Christ at his church. He challenged them, and they went with him out to this small village and started.

There was opposition, as usual, because the people don't

trust Christians. "You're just trying to force Christianity down our throats," was their attitude. As Bill said, it's stiff Hindu atmosphere there. But John just kept quietly working.

Now he has finished his third year there, and all kinds of good things have been happening. The government has been so pleased with the little school they started — it goes up to sixth grade now — that they are giving him permission to take it to eighth grade, and on up through high school if they do that successfully. They have had streetlights brought in, they have had a water tank put in, the roads have been hard topped instead of just mud, there's a building being built for a milk cooperative.

DB: What does that mean?

Bill: A milk cooperative is just a sales outlet for a group of dairy farmers. Instead of their competing against each other to sell their milk, they bring it all to this cooperative, which then has a wider market and can get them a more equitable return. Then they only have to do the milking and bring it in to the cooperative; the co-op then does the selling for them.

It's very beneficial, because it takes away that destructive selling competition through which a merchant can manipulate the farmers and use them against each other to increase his own profit. Now the profit goes to the people who are doing the work.

Joyce: At the building they are putting up, the milk will be processed, boiled, and put in plastic bags. They don't have the pasteurizing system we do, but it does the job. The milk is then put into plastic bags and sealed — just like a bag of peanuts. This is a great step forward for the farmers of that village.

So many things tie into this. Because the people were seen to be improving themselves, the banks are now giving them loans. The banks will lend to a person who is becoming literate before they'll give a loan to an illiterate.

They have this water tank now, a great big lovely water tank! That means more than just having a supply; it's better water, not water out of a muddy creek.

What they used to have was what are called in India "natural water tanks." That means tanks where water collects during the monsoons. That water is supposed to take care of washing, plus their buffalo and cows and the drinking water for their buffaloes and cows. The people take baths there in that water. They also defecate and so on in that water, as well as bathe. Everything imaginable goes on in that water, and they call them natural water tanks. We just call them a tank over there, and so we know what we're talking about. In dry season, it's dry. When the monsoon comes, of course, it slowly builds up. And the tank in this village had never been cleaned.

After John got them on the road to literacy and Jesus and self-improvement and self-respect, they got together as a team, and they went from the whole circumference all around right into the middle. They completely pulled up all the plants—there's a lotus that lives in places like that—and they took out bones, rocks, anything. That was the first time that municipal tank had ever been cleaned.

DB: Are these tanks metal? Concrete?

Joyce: No, they're natural, just ground, earth.

DB: Just a hole in the ground?

Joyce: It's just a low area where water collects.

Bill: Like a little lake, like a man-made lake.

Joyce: You can see how important it is for a community to have a clean lake that is a source of water, as well. That was another thing this Village Literacy Rehabilitation Project has done.

Bill: An additional benefit from all of this was that not only did they have a better tank and more water, better water, clean water, but now they had a healthier community, too. With all of the dirt and trash and pollution that had been going into that tank, it was causing a lot of sickness. Every year people were getting cholera, but now they had stopped the source of cholera and other water-borne diseases.

They also cut down the malaria, because now there were not the breeding spots for the mosquitoes, because they breed in stagnant water. They changed stagnant into usable water that was constantly being used and moved. So it had an effect that was much more widespread than just getting some clean water. It affected the whole health of that whole community.

*Joyce*: So you see a Village Literacy Rehabilitation Project has an impact and an outreach far beyond the simple literacy projects.

*DB*: Joyce, I'm guessing that in addition to all the people you know about who have learned how to read directly through your project, there may be thousands and thousands of others who have learned because your graduates have taught someone else—a neighbor, a cousin, or somebody else in the village. I remember years ago hearing that a man named Frank Laubach tried to tap that dynamic with his "Each One Teach One" slogan, because illiteracy was so widespread. I'm wondering whether you have heard of anything like that happening as a result of your various literacy programs.

*Joyce*: It's interesting you should mention that because we actually have it organized as another program, not just something we hope will happen now and then.

When International Literacy Year arrived, I asked the Bible League if they would give me a couple of thousand more to make it a special year. They said they couldn't.

So when I got on the plane going back to India, all the way over that night I was saying, "Lord, what can we do? I'm coming back, and my people are going to say, 'Oh, Ama, what can we do this year, because it's International Literacy Year?'" My heart seemed to have sunk almost as far down as from the plane to the ocean, and I thought, "Oh, what are we going to do?" Finally, I felt that the Lord was saying, "Start an intensive 'Each One Teach One' program." So I wrote myself some notes.

As soon as I arrived in India, I got together with my executive coordinator and my program coordinator. We were talking, and they said, "What are we going to do?" I said, "This is what we're going to do." "Never work," they said. "Yes, it will," I said. "How will it work?" they asked. I said, "I don't know, but we're going to start it."

And so we began. We laid out what we were going to do for our "Each One Teach One" program, which of course would be post literacy, the Post Literacy Class. We began to challenge all the graduates from the ten-month training to pick somebody, either in their family or a neighbor or whoever, to teach. So far we have over a hundred thousand who have been taught in that manner.

DB: A hundred thousand!

Joyce: Over a hundred thousand. We find that a mother will go back and teach her husband, or she'll teach a child. One lady wanted to come, and she was about sixty years old. She came, up in the Hindi area, and she was saying, "Oh, I must learn." She learned, and every day she would go back and teach her daughter. I said, "Why don't you bring your daughter?" "No, no, no, she has to help at home, but I want her to learn so that I can get her a better marriage alliance."

DB: Would her being able to read really make a difference in a marriage alliance?

Joyce: Oh, it makes a tremendous difference. This woman was studying to benefit herself, but the benefit was going to the daughter as well, so that she would get a good man who would have a literate wife.

And here's something else we sometimes find: the husband will object to his wife's plans to come to the classes. He'll say, "You can't go, you can't go, you stay home," and he's very bitter about it.

"Fine," she says, but she slips away and starts to learn. Then he begins to see changes in her.

"Oh, you're going to that class?" he says.

"Yes, I'm going."

"Well," he says, "you're doing better here, you're keeping the house clean, you're keeping the children clean, and you seem to be able to read some things," he says. He gets very happy, but he's illiterate himself. So then he goes with her to the classes. I heard recently that there was a whole family — father, mother and three children—who were attending the same village center to become literate.

DB: And does this have any wider impact?

Joyce: Oh, yes. We have heard about many, many women, dozens of women who apparently must have had some natural leadership ability. After they learn to read and write, when village elections have come around, they stand for office and get elected. They're not only elected to the village council, they're elected as council presidents. Every woman I know who has been elected to the council has been elected president of the council. So she leads the village.

Bill Teate: Tell him about the Hindu woman whose husband was literate, but she was not. Was it Sampoornamma?

Joyce: Oh, yes. Really, what has happened to this lady I call the triumph of God's grace. She was a Hindu woman who came to Christ, finished her one-year program of literacy, learned to read and write, and then was elected to be president of the village council. She led them into putting plans on paper and redesigning roads in that village, *pukkah* roads.

Bill: *Pukkah* means good.

Joyce: Yes, I mean good roads, you know, proper roads. They had to present this, of course, to the government, for permission. But she was the one who had done that all with the council, and down at the bottom was her signature. They sent me a copy of that to prove that here was this woman who had become president of the village council, and it was her authority that was causing this improvement in the village. She lived at Puvallim Badu, about thirty miles north of Madras.

Her husband was a little surprised by all this. He was literate, and so he had decided he didn't have to go to a literacy class, but he had encouraged her to do so. Before that, her life was just getting up every day, getting the children up, getting them washed, making them breakfast over some stones with a fire, and this and that, day after day, and not much to life at all. That changed after she attended our Village Literacy Rehabilitation Project classes for one year.

She had five children, and her husband actually was one of

the Project teachers, but she was not being taught by him. She attended one of the other classes there. When the village council was being elected in 1996, Sampoornamma had friends who encouraged her to enter the contest for the job as president, because she was qualified to read and write. So she won that election unanimously.

Then she got the roads, but that was just the beginning. Her story is very exciting to me; it gives me a terrific feeling because it is clear that God had already given her leadership ability that was just hidden inside her, just being held down. Latent, just being squashed, repressed. It was being strangled; no life could come to it.

In the course of her duties, she soon met the government man, who is called a Block Development Officer (BDO). Every district in India is divided up into blocks, and each one has a BDO. She began to bring to his attention, and to other authorities, various needs of the village. She was concerned about the welfare of the village.

As soon as she realized the power she had through her job to help other people, she began to utilize all the government programs and schemes she could find. She found some that I had never even heard of. She arranged for all the government programs she could find to help with the uplifting of the villagers and to bring that whole village into a completely new dimension of development.

DB: Of course, she never could have done any of that if she had not known how to read and write. Illiterate village councils could never get to know about the government programs.

Joyce: That's right, she never would have known about them. For instance, she helped to get a government contribution of 10,000 rupees for any poor girl in her village who got married. Did you know that was available, Bill?

Bill: None of us knew that. I didn't.

Joyce: I didn't know it either. But she had found that out, and she got it. And so the poor girls got 10,000 rupees—about

$350—toward their wedding, and the dowry, and so on, when they're going to get married. She got the support from the government for 150 streetlights, and for providing a proper cremation ground.

When a family with two daughters agreed to the government request to limit population growth by having no more children, since they had no son and no chance of having a son, she got for them the promise of a government grant of 20,000 rupees each—about $700 for each of their girls when they attain eighteen years of age, to help them make a good marriage. These are things I never heard of, but she found them out, and she began to tap these sources.

There are a lot of other things like that she did, and all because of her literacy and her warm heart of love for the people, since she had received the love of Jesus in her heart when she became a Christian after going through our Bible based literacy course.

She was able to get house loans, and loans to buy buffaloes, and she got help to run three primary schools. Can you imagine? Help to run a primary school! Three of them! Here she is, a neo-literate, not a graduate of a school, you see. She arranged for eye camps, for the doctors to come and take care of the eyes. She got money support from the government for digging wells for the villages. She got permission for fifty water taps, and many other things.

What a change in one woman's life! She is happy that she is instrumental in helping other women and her village people, but she knows that the root cause of it all is her coming to know the Lord Jesus Christ, who gave her a new heart and a new life.

I think the Lord must just stand up there and give a clap because of all that is happening, Don. What I see in all this is that we're offering them a substitute for their idols. I don't mean that Jesus is the substitute, really; the idols were the substitute, but now they are gone, because Jesus is coming into their lives.

# Village Literacy Rehabilitation Projects

**Bill:** We're offering the real thing.

**Joyce:** Yes. We're offering them the real thing, so that they can look at the whole system of idols and say, "I don't need that." And this is what I think: I think God must really love India, because the idols that were there, those substitutes for God, have been keeping the truth from them.

Let me say that we also are having what we call self-help programs. We have a man who knows how to produce about 200 different items that can be produced in a village in a home—shaving cream, detergent, tooth powder, bluing laundry, regular soap, a disinfectant they can make. So we have taken this man off his job as an Area Coordinator and brought him in to do this type of teaching. Now all the villages in our VLRP program are being taught every year how to have self-help programs, and that brings in more income for the family when they learn to read. They couldn't do these things without knowing how to read. I wish I had that list!

**DB:** You started with five of these Village Literacy Rehabilitation Projects. How many do you have running now?

**Joyce:** Thirty-four, and more planned. I have four in my files ready to be assigned, and many more in India waiting for us to process. We're ready to move into high gear on this. And we have had some dropouts; I'll be frank about that. In the seventh VLRP, the leadership went funky, and it took about a year before we could get somebody to go in and straighten them out.

**Bill:** As an Irishman, I would not know what *funky* is. But maybe Americans do.

**DB:** I'm not sure I could define it either, Bill. In music, it might sometimes be good, but probably not in a literacy project.

**Joyce:** It was way out in the boondocks, among the Santali tribes. There are about ten million Santali, and it took us about a year to find a replacement. Now it's going well again. If ever we find a serious problem, and sometimes we do, then we cut support for the person and hold the project in abeyance until we find a leader we can trust.

DB: Are you telling me that their private lives make a difference?

Joyce: Oh, yes.

DB: It's not politically correct to say that in America today!

Bill: These things are not easy anywhere. But we don't give up, and God has continued to supply fresh, dedicated people. Now the troubled projects are up and running again.

Joyce: Well, I feel morally, and before the Lord—I think those go together, though some may not—anyway, as the Director of this Literacy India Trust, I feel an obligation to see that the principles of Christian living as set in the Bible are carried out in all aspects of this program. I cannot sit by and not do anything when we see a moral problem.

We have also dismissed Area Coordinators. They are the liaison between the village classes and our office. One we dismissed for drinking, one for smoking and improperly using names that he got from us—trying to get extra money from those people—another man, just recently, for taking money for the Bibles that we send to give out as prizes to the new readers who have earned them after ten months. He was taking them and selling them for his prices, and so he's gone. I have no patience for that type of thing.

Bill: We've built moral and ethical values into the program.

DB: That's good to know, for people who support the work.

Bill: It's important to make this clear, because while we want to expand the work, there is no point in doing that if you lose its quality and purpose. So we are careful to recruit leaders on the principle of assessing successful performance in every way over a period of some years. Only those who meet those standards are invited into this program. In other words, the Village Literacy Rehabilitation Project program is so popular that we do not need to seek applications. We can select, and we are doing that at this point. That's a very good thing for people to know. I hardly realized it myself, until now. I knew it, but...

Bill Teate: I hardly realized it either!

Joyce: Getting back to the total number of projects that we

have going: the 34th has just been assigned. 33 are running, with a total of 442 classes running. There have been 1,066 classes completed, with 31,980 learners. Those are the latest figures I have as of January 1999. Now the goal we set at first was to reach fifty villages, which would be reaching at least 75,000 people. But in some classes, there are more than thirty, and in some places there are more than thirteen classes. The people are squeezing themselves in. So we are getting close to halfway to our first goal.

**Bill Teate:** I remember you telling me, Joyce, about one area where a start-up Village Literacy Rehabilitation Project was planning for roughly 390 literacy students per year, each year, for four years; they had 1500 who all wanted to start the first year!

**Joyce:** That's right. There's such a hunger for this! And the number of people who are coming to Christ is about the same average as we were finding with the original literacy classes, about 42%. One time I found it was 37%, another 45%. That means an average of at least one prayer cell for each class. And those prayer cells usually turn into churches.

**DB:** So as we look at this new program of Village Literacy Rehabilitation Projects, you have already seen about 12,000 new believers and 1000 potential new churches, with many more to be expected each year if the program is permitted to expand?

**Joyce:** Yes. The Lord has been good, and I want to say this to the glory of the Lord. In January of 1987, when I sat down for those ten nights and the Lord was saying to me, "Get this on paper," and He just gave me that whole program, never, ever did I feel or know at that point what the Lord was going to do with it. I thought that it probably would stay just within Andhra Pradesh or Tamilnadu, but less than a week ago I got a report from India saying that we have received 1,200 applications for new literacy projects, projects of the original ten-month variety with one class in each of five villages.

When we interview the applicants, we ask, "Why do you

want this?" They usually say "Because we want to get into this village for evangelism, and we cannot do it without literacy."

DB: So you have new pending applications from people who want to use your Jesus-based literacy materials to go into 6,000 villages?

Joyce: That's right. A Project Officer has five villages, times thirty individual learners in each village.

Bill: At least that.

Joyce: And this is happening although we have never advertised. We have 1200 applications to run the original Literacy Projects sitting there in the Madras office, right now, wanting, asking. People are coming saying, "Oh, I will do a good job!" So it's going to grow. God has taken His program, His design, and He is blessing it to the lives of tens of thousands in India.

DB: I'm trying to do some quick math here. This year you have 50,000 in those classes, and another 13,000 or so going through the twelve-month Jesus-based literacy classes in Village Literacy Rehabilitation Projects. At 40%, that means probably about 25,000 of those 63,000 people who have been learning about Jesus will be coming to put their trust in Him this year alone? In one year? And you have applications waiting to start classes that would teach another 180,000 in 6,000 new villages?

Joyce: There's nothing like it in India.

Bill: No there isn't. Now I feel that this is a program that is of God. It came to Joyce's mind, and she, of course, is a person that can organize well. She has organized it well, but I believe it is a program of God.

Joyce: Oh, I know it is. I am happy being His instrument.

Bill: I am very confident that we are doing God's work in this program, and doing it in God's way, because it's bringing so much blessing to so many people. We are looking to God for His provision, and the challenges are tremendous.

# Chapter 21
# The Status of Women

**D**B: When my father was in India visiting mission stations back in the 1930s, he was tremendously impressed with the work of Amy Carmichael, what she was doing to rescue unwanted children. He came back saying that boys were worth something at that time in India, but girls were not, and that the girl babies were often just drowned. Now, how are things in India for women today? Are they much better? A little bit better?

Joyce: They may be a little bit better. In the villages, girls who are not wanted are handed over to the Hindu temples to be used in temple prostitution. They still hand over boys too, but for a different reason. They hand over the girls because they don't want them, but they hand over their sons because boys are the most precious thing that they have. They'll offer a son at a very young age to the gods, to the temple, but then he goes in for male prostitution. That practice still continues.

That's what Amy Carmichael was dealing with: she was rescuing both boys and girls from the temples and from death. She was from Ireland, by the way.

Bill: Yes, an Irish girl!

Joyce: That sort of thing still happens today If a family keeps a girl child until she is at a marriageable age, they have to pay an outlandishly high dowry to the man who marries her. That's part of why female children are killed.

To fight that, the government is trying to challenge women to help remove poverty from their communities. So they want the women to learn to read and write. They say they want equality for women, to end the killing of girl babies, and to end malnutrition in children.

Another thing the government is doing to try to help women is teaching awareness about destructive diseases like AIDS. We include that sort of awareness training in our literacy program, as well as covering eye diseases, the dangers of drinking polluted water, and more.

Don, we know of three people who have recently come out of prostitution. One was a male prostitute and a pimp. Two were women in prostitution. When they studied our AIDS awareness material, they immediately left their "jobs" and started earning a living in proper, regular work. At least one of those women became a Christian.

DB: I'm surprised that India has not been more aggressive in defending women, since they had a woman president, Indira Gandhi. But during all the time of her political power, there wasn't much progress, really, for women in India, was there?

Joyce: This is an enigma about India. When the woman is on a certain level, from a certain socioeconomic status on up, she can be accepted and go any place, try for any political position, even to becoming the prime minister of the government. But from that threshold level down, women are nothing.

DB: So your literacy programs are really crucial for women?

Bill: That's right.

Bill Teate: They're bringing them up through that level.

Bill: That's right. And a quick interjection. Officially, the government of India, as Joyce has been sharing, has very aggressive programs to uplift women. But that's only on paper. They are effective for a certain segment of Indian women, the upper-level, urban sector. So you're talking about 10–15% of the women of India. These directives from the central government have no effect at all on the 85% of the women who are in the rural areas.

DB: But the literacy program does have an effect?

Bill: A tremendous effect! It breaks through apathy or whatever the obstacle may be, helping women through that invisible barrier that they need to be brought through. That's what we're sharing.

*Joyce:* Our program coordinator, who has her doctorate in adult education, was invited to speak at the launching of a big government literacy program on International Women's Day. All the learners were women, and all the teachers were women. She talked about the importance of women in the life of the village, in the life of the family. Let me read you part of her speech:

> Woman is the maker or breaker of the family, of the community, and of the nation. The enemy of the woman is the woman. Freedom will never come from the outside; freedom should come from within yourself. Do not expect somebody to hand over the freedom; you have to take it. Make yourself happy; only then you can make others happy. Previously, women were neglected, but now everybody has started to think about the women in the community. So be courageous, and start to achieve your freedom.

This is our feeling, you see. We're trying to encourage women, and the best way is helping them to get to know Jesus. In addition, of course, we are also teaching both men and women to become self-sufficient, to take up handcrafts of some sort, cottage crafts, small-scale industries, animal husbandry, anything constructive and useful.

In one area, the women were taught how to do cross-stitch embroidery. This was to help them earn an honest living or some extra income. It has turned into a big program through something Bill did.

*Bill:* Well, the quality impressed me so much that I brought some of their work back to the States with me, and people I have met here who do cross-stitch work are amazed at the quality of what these ladies do.

*DB:* Yes, I've seen it, and my wife does beautiful cross-stitch work, but when we looked at your cross-stitching from

India and at the back of their work, we were both struck with the high quality.

Bill: It is. And it is very moving when you know that many of the women who do it are rescued from the streets. Their home has been the street, and their living has been the sale of their bodies. It seems that God releases some inherent skill that has been there, and these women are able to do these cross-stitch pieces. Now we've got towels and napkins and wall plaques, all done in beautiful cross-stitch work.

Well, the women were doing this work as they were being taught, but the bottleneck was sales. They could not market these things, because naturally, in a village setting, there are practically no homes that could use this type of material. They needed to sell in the cities, which they did a little. But I realized, very quickly, that this program would fail unless a good sales outlet was developed. We helped them to develop sales outlets in India through large stores in the cities, and these materials go very well there. But that still was not sufficient to take care of the hundreds of ladies who were doing this and were dependent upon this to feed their families.

So I started to bring them back to America, and then to show them...

Bill Teate: In his suitcase!

Bill: Yes, in my suitcases. I brought an extra suitcase in order to bring a suitcase full. I was advancing money from our own funds to pay these women, so that we would not have them going without food for their families. At first we were having minor sales, relatively minor sales. I was hardly breaking even, just selling enough for me to go back and buy some more. We were building up a small stock, because to develop a market outlet, even in America, is not easy, and I was only doing it as I was going to conferences. Even there I was hesitant to push it.

Then our good friend, Bill Teate, came into the picture. He saw the pieces and got excited about hearing the potential of each of these towels: a towel with a cross-stitch design on it that sells for $3.00, would support a family for a day; a wall plaque that sells for $10.00 would support a family with basic food for three days; and a $15.00 wall plaque would support a family for five days.

Joyce: These wall plaques have Scriptures on them. That's what caught Bill Teate's heart and mind and imagination. They were more than just pretty designs. They had Scripture on them, too.

Bill: Yes. So Bill Teate got excited about it, and he started showing to friends. In a year he doubled our sales. But that was still relatively small, because he doubled them from almost nothing. That's not terrifically significant. But this past year was a phenomenal year of growth.

We give thanks where thanks is due, and that is to my friend Bill Teate. Bill himself has told me that it is not his ability at selling, although Bill is a good salesman. But he has told me again and again that as he sees this, it is not his ability at selling, but it is God's working and moving in the hearts of people.

To us this confirms again that if you do God's ministry in God's way, God will supply what is needed. In this instance, He's supplying the market and the sales. And when the market and the sales increase, we can get more and more women of India able to emerge from immorality and support themselves in a moral way.

DB: How do you handle this financially? Is it done as part of the mission?

Bill: No. The profits go to the mission, if there are any profits; but we do not operate this for profit. We run it to get the maximum volume so as to help more women. So we set it up as a single proprietorship called Joy-S Associates, registered in the name of my wife, Joyce. It is a ministry through a single proprietorship. We pay state sales taxes and run it basically at cost.

If we ever made a profit, that profit would go back into ministry. This last year is the first year we did make a profit. I just told my wife as we were coming here yesterday, "Joyce, you're going to have to pay taxes this year." It was also was the first year we had to ship supplies from India because I couldn't carry enough. So everything I carried was sold, and in addition we're having to ship packets upon packets, because of the sales that are being done through our good friend, Bill Teate.

DB: How did you do it, Bill?

Bill Teate: It has simply been a work of God. In my normal work, I visit many churches, and I challenge them to sponsor literacy classes or to sponsor a church planter in India or to print Bibles. I simply thought, "Well, maybe I could make some of these available."

I never dreamed that when, in one church for example, I put some of these Scripture wall hangings and some of these hand towels on a table, that the women came out from the sanctuary and literally mobbed the table. A frenzy, every time!

And God has raised up helpers, especially Betty Foster, the wife of a retired Methodist minister. I think she's the best organist and pianist in the state of Delaware. She travels to many churches, leading praise times for women by her playing and her sharing. God simply touched her heart with these cross-stitch items, and she said, "I will take them wherever I go." She is now selling $100 a week! This from a woman who is the wife of an 80-year-old retired Methodist minister. She is on fire, and I'm just sitting back and watching God do this through people that He is raising up.

Bill: And another thing to add, is that through Joy-S we are now also starting to market work that is done with leather. So we have leatherwork with women's purses and men's wallets, and leather Bible cases.

Other classes are teaching women to do embroidery rather than cross-stitch on towels and tablecloths. Whatever these ladies make, we'll try to market, because we're talking about rehabilitating, not just hundreds of ladies, but thousands, and tens of thousands of ladies every year.

They are becoming productive citizens of their community. We encourage them to do something that is marketable in

India, and they do that. These things are also marketable in India. But then we get to such a volume, because of the number of families involved, that they do not have a market in India that can use all of that. And so we are encouraging export.

Another factor is that the government of India is very favorable toward exported materials, so this gives these women a higher status in the economic society of India. They are people who are producing materials that are exportable. That gives them favor with the government. So there are a lot of things that are produced in India and that are sold through Joy-S. Joy-S is legally a for-profit single proprietorship, but it really is a part of the ministry. Our purpose in this is not to make profit, but to increase volume of distribution, because every single piece distributed contributes to a family fed and a family rehabilitated.

Bill Teate: I would like to stress once again that what first caught my attention was this: the first item I saw was a Scripture wall hanging: *"My soul finds rest in God alone; my salvation comes from him"* (Psalm 62:1 NIV).

Bill: Right.

Bill Teate: Going back to the very basic ministry of India Bible Literature, the distribution of the Word of God, I thought how that Deuteronomy says we should be talking about the Word when we get up, when we go to bed, wherever we go. And it should be in our homes.

I thought, "How wonderful! This is another way of getting the Word of God out. It will not only help these women in India, but Christians in America who meditate on the Word of God when they see it! They can hang these up at home; they can put them on their office walls. This can be a testimony and a witness, because the Word of God is powerful, whether it's in the Bible, whether it's spoken, or whether it's on a plaque on a wall!"

DB: I know many of my congregation who would do well to look every day at a verse that says, "My soul finds rest in God alone," and every other pastor in America must feel the same way.

Bill: Even a motel like this. Maybe we can get this man to put one in each room!

* * * * *

At that point there was a general cheer, and the conversation dissolved into a brainstorming session about how to get these beautiful cross-stitch Scripture wall plaques into the hands and before the eyes of more and more Americans.

# Chapter 22

# The Impact Outside of India

Dr. C. S. Lewis once wrote that God does "all things for each." Nothing helps one without helping everyone else at the same time. Just as when one member of the body suffers, all members suffer, so too when God is blessing one part of the world, it is possible for other parts to enter into the blessing and experience blessing of their own through participation.

This certainly has been true of the way God has blessed the work of Bill and Joyce Scott in India. In talking with them and with their friends in the United States, I have heard many amazing and inspiring stories about the impact that the work in India has had on churches and on individuals outside India. I should not have been surprised. Whenever we help, we are helped.

You can grasp the full beauty of these stories more easily if we back up a couple of steps. We need to explain the links between the work in India and Christian churches and individuals outside India. Call to mind the amazing spread of the Christian faith in its early years, for that is where Bill and Joyce looked for inspiration and instruction as they designed their work in India. They looked to the Bible, and studied Paul's missionary methods.

## Paul's Church Planting Strategy

Everyone knows that Paul was a great evangelist. He founded churches in areas where the Gospel had never been preached before. But that is only part of the story. The really impressive fact is that he founded churches that lasted, churches that grew strong and spread, churches that survived and thrived without financial support from the mature churches back in Jerusalem and Antioch.

How did that happen? The answer is that Paul was far more than an evangelist. When he founded a church, he did not just go into a town, win some converts, and then go on to start another church somewhere else. He knew that would not work.

After winning men and women to Christ, Paul stayed and spent time with them. He taught them. He selected leaders and trained them to select and train other leaders. Sometimes he would spend as much as two years at a time in a place. Then they were ready for the three tasks of any church: to be self-sustaining, to be self-perpetuating into the next generation, and to plant other churches by winning converts from the people among whom they lived.

Third, he would follow up. He would stay in touch with their leaders and remain aware of their situation. He would come back for visits and spend more time with them. He would write them letters. If there were specific problems, he would address them.

The fourth important element in Paul's strategy was to multiply himself by choosing and training key assistants who could in turn train others: men like Timothy and Titus, other men and women whom he named in his letters as fellow workers, and probably many more he never named. These assistants were often sent to visit the churches and help them to continue growing.

We do not know by name many of the men and women those assistants trained, but we do see a pattern for growth that looks very much like the growth of a vine. Jesus is the vine; we are the branches. Each branch, as it grows, is capable of sending out smaller branches, which can grow so that they in turn can send out new branches. And so it goes, spreading and growing.

## The Great Commission

This strategy should not surprise us. It is inherent in the Great Commission which Jesus gave his disciples before his ascension, and there is no doubt that he gave similar revelation and instructions to Paul. Look carefully and you will see that they establish a chain:

> *Go ye therefore, and teach all nations, baptizing them in the name of the Father, and of the Son, and of the Holy Ghost: Teaching them to observe all things whatsoever I have commanded you: and, lo, I am with you alway, even unto the end of the world. Amen.* (Matthew 28:19–20 KJV)

New disciples were to be taught to observe all the commandments of Jesus, including the commandment to make new disciples and make sure that they in turn would pass on these same instructions, and so keep the chain of conversion and teaching going, even to the end of the age.

The Bible shows us that the great results of Paul's work were linked to the mature churches back in Jerusalem and Antioch. It is from those churches that Ananias came, who healed Paul's blindness and confirmed his call. It is from those churches that Barnabas came, he who first introduced Paul to the fellowship of other believers. It is from those churches that Silas came, and John Mark, and Luke. All of these played key roles in his missionary activities.

Paul worked as a tentmaker in order not to be a financial burden on the new young churches, but he also had some initial support from the church in Antioch. Then when the church he planted at Philippi grew, he accepted some support from them to help him train those in other towns who would become church leaders and church planters.

The work of Bill and Joyce Scott in India has progressed along those lines. Following Paul's pattern, adapting it to local conditions, they have helped to connect mature churches in other nations with such training programs. Keep in mind that the men who go through this training come out prepared not only to plant self-sustaining churches, but to do it without being paid from overseas.

## A Philadelphia Story

This has had a dramatic impact not only on the work in India, but also on many churches outside India when they hear about it. One of the most moving stories is about the New Testament Church of Christ in Philadelphia.

Rev. Bill Teate, who for years has helped raise money in the US for the work of the Scotts, had been attending ACMC meetings since 1979. ACMC was founded to help churches in the United States be more effective in missions outreach. They work to help church missions committees learn how to raise missions awareness in a congregation, how to put on a missions conference, how to choose what missions organizations to give to, how to take care of missionaries when they come home on furlough, and so on.

Bill had a display booth at the 1994 Philadelphia convention of ACMC, handing out information about what the Scotts were doing. It was supposed to close at 4:00 on the second day, but it ran long. Let him pick up the story in his own words.

Bill Teate: I felt I didn't want to stay any longer, so I closed my booth down, and I inadvertently left one piece of literature on a table that was now bare. The display was gone. Everything was gone. I was gone.

The meeting closed, and while leaving, an inner-city pastor by the name of Nathaniel Winslow walked past the table, and he saw this one piece of literature. It was a brochure that tells how the money we raise is used twice. It prints Scriptures first, and then the money that's obtained from that is used to train church planters. It tells how the church planters are taught to be self-supporting. He was impressed by the fact that this gave dignity to these evangelists, and also by the fact that the

Scriptures are purchased by the people, not just given away. So there's dignity there, too.

Being an inner-city pastor, dealing with poor people, Nathaniel Winslow immediately picked up on the way this provided for the Gospel to be spread with dignity, both for those who heard it and for the indigenous evangelists who preached it.

He read that brochure, and about a month later he wrote to me. I phoned him, and his words to me were, "As I stood at that table and read that brochure, the Holy Spirit went through me like an electric shock." And he said, "This was the missions strategy that I had dreamed of years earlier, the principles. Why doesn't somebody do it this way? And now I saw that there was a strategy in existence, in operation, exactly what God had laid on my heart." And he said, "This is what we want to get behind."

So he asked me how his church could sponsor the training of a church planter, where all these elements in the strategy would occur. I said, "Well, there's a $5,000 ministry package, and it includes a year of training and equipping for a church planter, 500 Bibles, 50 New Testaments, 1,000 Scripture gift packs, 1,000 children taught in a two-week-long Vacation Bible School, and a ten-month adult literacy class for 30 people of whom an average of 12 become Christians. We give churches up to a maximum of four years to come up with that."

He said, "I think we could do $1200 a year, so that in four years we could underwrite our own church planter sponsorship."

And I thought that would be exciting, coming from what was probably a rather poor inner-city church. So I said, "I think that's wonderful."

So he said, "I'm going to make a commitment that in four years we'll raise $5,000 and do a church planter sponsorship."

The ACMC meeting was in March, and this conversation was in April. In May, God brought us our first matching fund opportunity. The foundation gave us the conditions, and one of them was that they would match any individual gift of $100 or more. Now frankly I thought it was foolish to tell Nathaniel Winslow, because I thought none of the poor people of his inner-city church would have $100 at a time to give. So why even bother? But I phoned him, and in spite of my logic, I told him, because I was so excited about this matching fund arrangement. And he said, "I am excited to know this; we'll take advantage of it." And he said, "Are you available the first Saturday in November [1994] to come and speak at our missions conference? With matching funds, I would like to raise $2500 by November so we could have a church planter in about eight months instead of four years."

And I said, "Yes, the date is open. I will come."

So he began sending me checks. Some of them were rumpled, but they were all $100, each qualifying for matching funds. They kept coming and kept coming and kept coming, and instead of having $2500 qualifying for matching by November, they had it by August. So I assigned them their first church planter sponsorship.

But that was not all. Nathaniel Winslow kept surprising me. Every time I would call him, he would surprise me. When I called him in August, I said, "Praise the Lord, you've got your first church planter sponsorship."

"That's right, and now I would like to have a second one by November when you come, instead of our first one."

I said, "This is amazing!"

He said, "God's going to do it! God has laid this on my heart! I've been waiting for this for years!"

So November came, and I came to the conference. Now, my job is calling on pastors and presenting these opportunities and persuading them to take part in them. But I had never called on Nathaniel Winslow. I had never met him face-to-face until I went to his missions conference in November. God had worked in his heart without any persuasion from me.

When I went in November to his church on Chestnut Street in West Philadelphia, I discovered a building with two levels. I went upstairs, and there were about 25 people gathered for their missions conference. With most churches, the frustration is, I never have enough time. They always give me 15 or 20 minutes and it's hard to share in that time. And I said to him, "How much time do I have?"

He said, "You have an hour and a half." So I was thrilled!

I took the whole hour and a half, and they were excited by what was happening among the poor in India. I told them of the literacy work and how it uplifted the people who were hurting economically and who needed health care, and couldn't read and write, and how they got the Gospel at the same time as they learned to read.

Later Nathaniel Winslow said to me, "I believe that could be an answer to the poor here in America. It could be a ministry for inner-city churches throughout America. Could Joyce Scott come next year and share some of these principles? We've got a high school teacher in our congregation that could maybe take some of this and begin to use it, designing literacy programs that not only teach people to read and write but also teach the Gospel, and better health, better finance, and so forth." And we have begun to explore that.

But getting back to that conference, when I was finished Nathaniel Winslow stood up. He said, "God's going to do a great miracle tomorrow morning when we take our commitments to India." This was the first Saturday in November. He said, "I've been needing a new car, and I'd saved up $5,000 for that car. It was a used car but in good condition, and I figured it would definitely cost $5,000. But I was able to get that car for $2,500. It was a miracle." And he said, "God, I know why I saved up $5,000. The other $2,500 is for India, so when it's matched, I can do a whole church planter sponsorship myself," and as he said that, he broke down. He didn't weep out loud, he just couldn't talk, and he just put his head down.

I was so moved.

I get so sick of the kind of Christianity that's just talk: "Oh, we have such a burden for the inner-city," and "We're so burdened for the disadvantaged." But when Nathaniel Winslow took that money he had saved to buy that used car, he was obviously, as the Bible teaches, giving sacrificially, not out of his abundance like the rich and middle-class churches I call on, but out of his need. And God was moving him to do it.

I was so moved by that, I got up from my seat, I went up, and I threw my arms around him. I said, "Brother Winslow, I want you to know I love you." I don't say that type of thing lightly. I turned around to the 25-member group there, and I said, "I'm deeply moved with what your pastor has done. We're having elections next week. And I want you to know that the answer to our poverty problems is not political, and it's not financial. The answer is Jesus."

Then the pastor went on to say, "My son was going to spend $200 on music, and he went out twice to buy the music, and he said, 'Dad, I can't find the music. God won't let me spend this, and it's because this $200 is for India,'" and that got matched, and that became $400, that was $400 more.

Well, the end result was that by November 30th that poor inner-city church had given over $14,000 that qualified for matching. That made a total for India of $28,000 after it was matched. So they had five church planters they sent out, and they're working on their sixth one. They sent out five church planters in eight months instead of one in four years!

After this was all over, I talked to him in January 1995, and he said, "Could you get Bill and Joyce here at our missions conference the first Saturday in June?"

I said, "I will try." I was sure they would if they could fit it into their schedule, because I knew them and how they live in the villages of India. Bill has often said to me that what excites him is not the big money gifts we get from what we call major donors, $50,000 gifts and $100,000 gifts, but the gifts that come from people who give sacrificially. He always cares more for the $5 and $10 gifts. He has always told me that. I think it comes from his background as a poor boy in Ireland, probably.

So Brother Winslow said to me, "I'll tell you why I would like to have them come," he said. "Since we've raised $14,000 matched, that's $28,000. I want to raise another $36,000 so we'll have $50,000 in cash, qualifying for matching funds. When that is matched, it will be a $100,000, and we can do a whole million people unit area in India, teaching twenty master church planters to be trained and equipped to go out for a lifetime of self-supporting ministry."

Can you imagine that? In 22 years of doing this work, I have never thought there was any sense in visiting inner-city churches. First, in my mind, they have no money. And secondly, I was talking to another pastor who said that an inner-city pastor told him such churches just don't give to missions. He said they're not trained to give to missions. So I thought there was no reason to go.

I'm being honest with you. On my own, I never would have taken the initiative to go to an inner city church. And now it looks like God is going to do a whole million people unit from a relatively small, inner-city church! God is just doing miracles that are astounding on the fund-raising side here at the very same time doors are opening in India as they never have before.

That's just one story.

Just as God has been doing incredible miracles in India for this ministry to occur, I am seeing that He is doing just as incredible miracles here, to show us that this is His work. And God is getting the glory. The funding that is needed is not being raised through slick fund-raising methods that are really of the flesh. God is doing miracles here raising up the funding necessary, just as He's doing miracles for the actual work to happen in India.

And by the way, Bill and Joyce were scheduled to go to that church for their Missions Conference in June, and they were given four hours to speak! From one to five on a Saturday afternoon! If more American churches did that, maybe more people would get excited.

DB: It's impossible not to get excited, just hearing about it. But raising another $36,000! That seems incredible when you are talking about a poor church with just about seventy members. That would mean an average of about $500 per member!

Bill Teate: Well, Pastor Winslow is building up to it. He wants to prepare between January and June. He says he's well-connected with inner-city people. So some money is coming from Camden, across the river in New Jersey. I've gotten checks from Camden. It's not all going to come from his church. The challenge is spreading! And that's even more exciting. To have a dream like that takes a lot of faith.

DB: Maybe it is easier to reach the hearts of the poor than the hearts of the rich.

Bill Teate: Well actually, and this is very interesting, the story of what God is doing in India through the Scotts is reaching both! I can tell you a story just as miraculous, in its own way, about something that happened in one of the most affluent churches I've ever worked with, the Scottsdale Bible Church in Phoenix, Arizona. They have 4,000 people coming every Sunday morning.

I went to visit them in the early 1980s, wanting to challenge them to do one of our "multiplication plan" projects, but they felt that was a little too bizarre. They are quite conservative. But one of their elders, Dale Micetic, went to India and saw the work first-hand, and through his influence they put the mission work in India into their extended missions budget for $500 a month.

That went on for a number of years. Then they called a new missions pastor, Gil Crowell. He came in the early 1990s, and I started talking with him. A couple of years later, he went to India with us and saw for himself the work being done. Everybody who goes to India with us comes back saying, "I can't believe the cost-effectiveness, the bang for the buck, how much is happening the way Bill Scott has set this up."

They get excited seeing that the money is used twice: first going into the printing of the Scriptures, and then the proceeds from the sale of Scriptures being used to train church planters, teaching them to be self-supporting for the rest of their lives, and it just keeps on working and never stops.

So he was very impressed and wanted to do something significant. I explained the "multiplication plan" to him, and he was able to pass that vision on to the Scottsdale church. Now they were open and ready to receive it.

They have a Saturday night service and two Sunday morning services, with a total attendance of 4,000 in those weekend services. We expected they might have about 3,000 people who would participate. So we did the regular routine: we sent them a check for $30,000, to be given out in $10 bills with no records kept.

DB: You gave this rich church $30,000?

Bill Teate: Yes, and they actually gave out $24,500. They sent us back the $5,500. That was the last weekend in January, 1995. Now there are two professional women golfers who belong to that church, Betsy King and Barb Thomas. They are good friends, and when they go on tour, they room together. Betsy King is very famous, but Barb Thomas had never won a tournament even though she had been a professional for twelve years. So she was not well-known.

Well, on the Sunday in January when the money was given out, Barb Thomas was there. She got a ten-dollar bill to invest for God, just like everybody else, and she told us that the Lord laid on her heart, "Use this to register for the next LPGA tournament, as part of your registration fee." So she determined that if she won any money in that tournament she would tithe it to this project. She said "I'll give 10% of what I win back to God for India, and I'll use my ten-dollar bill as part of my registration fee."

She played that tournament three weeks after the launch of the multiplication plan. That would be about the third week of February 1995. And the next Monday morning *USA Today* ran a headline: "Barb Thomas wins LPGA golf tournament." After her victory, she told the reporters all about this, and the part that India played in her first LPGA tournament victory in twelve years on the tour.

Would you believe it? A great story like that and *USA To-day* never told a bit of it. But the local Phoenix newspaper did.

God touched the heart of an LPGA golfer, Barb Thomas, and helped her to win the tournament. I say He helped her to win, because all good things come from God! So she got a purse of $82,500 and tithed 10% of that, more than $8,000. And that came from a $10 bill in our multiplication plan project. From the whole project in that church over $108,000 came in.

So you see God is working in wealthy churches, and in inner-city churches, and in churches in between like yours, Don. He's working all over America at the same time as He's doing things in India like He's never done before.

There's another nice story out of that Scottsdale Bible Church multiplication project. Another member there is a professional baseball player who won the Rookie of the Year award in the American League in 1993. He pronounces his name Samen, but it's spelled like the fish, Salmon. He got a $10 bill, and do you know what he did with it? People are wonderfully imaginative! He used his $10 to rent a batting cage, and he said to a bunch of kids of Scottsdale, I'll give an hour's free batting instruction.

This is the Rookie of the Year! He plays for the California Angels in the American League. He would give a free hour of batting instruction in the batting cage to any teenager whose name was pulled out of a hat. They put a bunch of names in a hat, and he pulled one out. He said, "What I would like you kids to do is give a love offering for the Gospel to be spread in India, as a result of all this," and he got something like $54 from the love offerings of those kids. So he multiplied his seed money from $10 to $54, using his talents and abilities that God has given him.

DB: You know, I love that multiplication project idea. We had a great experience with it in our medium-sized, somewhere-in-the-economic-middle church. I remember some kids bought lemonade mix and sold lemonade—we were running our project in the spring—and another family put on dinners to benefit the mission work in India. Several ladies did craft projects, buying materials and selling what they made. One woman who made many of her own clothes bought fabric and made children's dresses to order. One bought wool and knitted sweaters to order. Two or three bought ingredients and made baked goods for sale. A retired man who had repaired golf clubs for a living went back to repairing golf clubs for the three months of the project and donated the proceeds. A piano teacher placed an ad for students and for the three months donated all she earned from those who answered that ad.

Bill Teate: That's the kind of thing people are doing all over America, and sometimes God intervenes in a special way to multiply the multiplication! I remember a man in the auto parts business who stocked one bin with one particular kind of small part with his $10, reinvesting the profits into that item. Well, sales on that particular item suddenly doubled. He was so startled that after a month he switched bin numbers, and put the money into stocking another item. Well, sales on the first dropped back to normal, and sales on the new item went way up. He made a lot of money for India, and he became convinced that God really wanted the work in India to be well supported.

DB: You know, Bill, I found in my church what you told me in advance: that the benefit to my congregation from their changed ideas about stewardship would be as great as the benefit to India.

Bill Teate: We've found that true everywhere we have done this multiplication project. The idea of working with money that is handed to them, not money they think they have made on their own, reminds people that everything we have comes from God, and they get a fresh understanding of what it really means to be stewards, custodians, trustees, of resources that come from God, including our health, our imagination, whatever.

DB: I am just as impressed, Bill, with another idea you came up with—not a gimmick dreamed up by some American fundraiser, but an idea that grew out of the actual experience of the church in India — the rice bag idea.

Bill Teate: It really has been another miraculous way that God is working right now. It started in the very poor villages where there are Christians. Money is really scarce, so what a lot of the Christian families do is that when the woman makes the meal at night, she'll take a handful of rice out before cooking for the family, and they have a rice pot, and they say "That's for Jesus," and they put a handful of rice in that pot each night.

This is a method God has raised up for funding poor churches in village India through little rice pots. When that pot is full, they take it to church. Literally, they take that rice pot to church and give it to the church, and they'll say that's their offering. The church sells the rice and uses the money for ministry. So we got a little "rice bag" made up, and we're challenging American Christians to fill those rice pots. Not with rice, of course, but with loose change, just as those extra grains of rice in the poor village are like loose change to us, something you can easily spare. The bags are small, just a few inches, and filled with ordinary mixed loose change they can hold about $30.

This was something that appealed particularly to a church that had a big building project and felt that they couldn't think about giving money to India or raising money for India. It was Christ Community Church in West Chester, Pennsylvania. The pastor is Jim Stevens. When we suggested a "multiplication project," he said, "I'd better wait, because we just built a new building, and we have a big building debt." I said, "I think you ought to go to India now and see what the Scotts are doing, and we'll worry about raising money for the work later."

So he went. Now, they had been wanting to put us into their budget for six years, but it didn't happen because of this huge building debt. I think they're working under restrictions from the bank as to how they can use their money.

Then God raised up this rice bag project. I was talking to the missions chairman, Tony Proto, who said, "By the way, we just missed getting in the budget again this year because of the building debt." I said, "Any chance of just giving these rice bags out and people filling them with loose change for a six or eight week period?" He said, "I love that idea."

So they gave out rice bags, and we've got a matching fund now for every rice bag filled with $30 or more, and we've got a goal of seeing 420 rice bags filled. This church has about 1100 people. This would be for a Village Literacy Rehabilitation Project. If they can fill 420 rice bags, and they all get matched, that would be $25,000, which will rehabilitate a whole village over four years, raising the level of that village, raising their economy, improving health, teaching the people to read and write. Most importantly, they get the Gospel, and some house churches are raised up.

And so it might be that just through this rice bag and the matching fund—which are both totally of God—right at this moment in time, a church that couldn't do anything because of budget constraints and other commitments could generate possibly $25,000 over four years. Now to me, from a fund-raising standpoint, that's a miracle.

DB: From my perspective as a pastor, Bill, it's a double whammy kind of miracle: one for India, and the other for the people in the church who experience a wonderful sense of partnership with the evangelists who are on the frontlines, seeing lives and even whole villages changed as they share the Gospel with people who live in darkness.

## Chapter 23
# "God Opening India"

**D**B: Bill, in explaining the success that you and Joyce have had with India Bible Literature, with Vacation Bible Schools for children, with the Schools of Evangelism that train church planters, and with all the other aspects of your work, several times you have used the phrase: "God opening up India." Now this phrase gives rise to two big questions: Just what happened? And why did it happen? And these questions have important theological implications.

Certainly the Bible is clear in saying that God never plays favorites; He *"shows no partiality"* (Acts 10:34 NKJV), He wants *"all men to be saved"* (1 Timothy 2:4), and He is *"not willing that any should perish"* (2 Peter 3:9). Those are quotations from Paul and Peter, and John quotes for us the words of Jesus when He said, *"God sent not His son into the world to condemn the world, but that the world through him might be saved"* (John 3:17). Jesus also said He came, *"to seek and to save that which was lost"* (Luke 19:10), and that surely includes Iraq and Iran and China and Africa and Sweden and Russia, as well as India.

God also says that if we turn to Him, He will turn to us. There are instances in the history of revivals that some have called "a nation turning to God." Could you tell us how you see the last fifty years in India in the light of these questions?

Bill: In retrospect, as I look at India, when we went there in 1950 as missionaries, it was basically an unknown country, a closed country. There was good mission work happening, but nothing spectacular. And as I shared with you in terms of distribution, we were struggling to get a few thousand pieces a year distributed. So India was basically closed. I see the era of the 1970s, and particularly the mid-seventies, as a time when God miraculously opened up India to the Gospel.

Let me share two stories in two areas. One is in the area of Scripture distribution; the other is in the area of evangelism.

First, during the years I was struggling in the area of Scripture distribution, there was another very dear man of God, who has now gone to be with the Lord, an Indian brother, who visited me frequently. He had the same burden that I had, to get the Word of God to the nation of India. God gave an identical vision to him as the one He gave to me. So this man and I were very close together in our thinking and in our partnership, of getting God's Word to India.

He would come to me to get Scriptures that he was distributing, and he was having the same problems that I was having, that people wouldn't accept him. His burden was more to get them into institutions—hospitals, schools, prisons, and the like—and he met the same resistance that I had going out into the villages. So we would share together.

One day this man of God came to me in my office, and he didn't know it, and I didn't know it, but this was his last visit before he went home to be with the Lord. It was in the 'seventies, and he came in my office and threw his arms around me, and my arms were around him. I felt his hot tears on my cheeks, and they then mingled with mine, because both of us were weeping, not because of sorrow, but because there was a joy that he could not express and I could not express either, a joy in what we saw was happening. This man of God looked at me and said, "Brother Bill, it is now happening. We are now seeing God opening this nation, that every home will have the Word of God. We're seeing it. We're going to live to see that day." And we were weeping because the people were coming to us to get the Word of God instead of our going to them.

He said, "Now, I'm not coming for a dozen Scriptures, I'm coming for thousands. And those are not enough for the people that are asking for them. Now they're coming and pleading with me. Muslims, Hindus, Parsees, non-Christians, pleading with me to get the Word of God."

I said, "That's the same with me. All the homes in the villages are open, and they're pleading, 'Come,' and if we don't go there, they're coming to us."

He said, "Brother Bill, this is God's answer to prayer." He did not live to see the fulfillment. I'm living and seeing the fulfillment now. That was God opening up, and he, this man of God, acknowledged with me that God has done a miracle.

DB: So your friend saw it as an answer to prayer.

Bill: Yes, like many great revivals. I don't think the church in America realizes the miracle that God has been doing in India. I've also tried to explain it in terms of what happened politically, talking about the time it took for people to realize that they had freedom, but that may not be the explanation. I believe that in 1975, when that man of God and I met, I believe we didn't realize it at the time, but that was the beginning of the opening of India to the Word of God so that today we're doing what we're doing. That's in the area of distribution.

DB: And you were praying for India, too, of course?

Bill: Oh, yes, and in the area of evangelism, a lot of things were happening. Young fellows that I had trained were now coming to me. And remember, in the 1950s I couldn't find one evangelist to go out with me to do ministry. I was taking school boys. In the 1960s, very few. In the 1970s, evangelists seemed to be coming out of the wall. How did that happen? There's only one explanation. God was working; God was moving. He was sending laborers into the harvest. These young fellows were coming with me. Some of them were graduates of that school in Pedapalli, the fruit of that work.

Two stories are now in my mind about it, and maybe I should share both of them, because they're both about what happened in tribal evangelism. One man who came was an associate pastor in a large church in Warangal. The senior pastor always asked me to bring the message in Telugu when I was in the area, which I did.

One time when I was there, having dinner with them, this

associate pastor said, "Sir, I want to speak to you alone." And when he came he said, "God has given me a burden for a tribal group," and he named the tribal group in Andhra. He said, "I have a burden to reach this group."

I said, "That's an unreached tribal group."

He said, "I know," he said, "but I have a burden. Will you come with me to see the place?"

I said, "All right," and I arranged it. I'm not sure whether I went that same weekend and stayed an extra day or came back. But I went with him. We walked into the jungle where these people were. I'm trying to get their name, because the other tribal group's name is in my mind. But we went into the jungle where this tribal group was, unreached, totally unreached. Not one single Christian that we knew of in this tribal group.

We knew that, as we walked through the jungle, people were watching us. These were not a primitive group; they wore clothing and so on. But they were very secretive. They wouldn't come out and talk to us, and he and I walked through that group, and we prayed.

We said, "Dear God, open up this area to the Gospel of Jesus Christ. You've given a burden to this young man, this young pastor. Fulfill that burden and vision," and we claimed in God's name, a church in this area, as we walked through that jungle.

Well, this man resigned from a very nice position as associate pastor in a large church. He went as a missionary to that group, to preach the Gospel. He lived with them in a little hut. He ate their food, which was obnoxious even to Indians, but he ate it. He lived the way they lived, no table, no chair; he sat on the ground. I went to visit him frequently, and we would go out among the people. He learned their language, which was related to Telugu, derived from it, but it was different, a dialect. I couldn't speak the tribal language. He learned it.

One year later, I was invited to the same place to dedicate the first church in that area, the very first church. There was now a group of baptized believers, just one year later. I went there, and they asked me to give the message, which I was going to give in Telugu. This evangelist was translating it into the tribal language. And I went.

The church, I looked for a building to dedicate. When they tell you, "Come dedicate a church," you look for a building. I saw no building, but I did see a clearing that wasn't there when we first went through, a place where they had cleared some trees. They had an area maybe about 100 feet by 30 feet that was cleared. We went there, and then they brought out woven mats that these tribal people made, and they put woven mats on the ground in that cleared area, and that was the church.

In fact, a boy ran across it, and somebody slapped him over the head, and said, "Don't be running in church." He sat down for the rest of the day. He didn't move!

That was the church that I dedicated. Beautiful! I mean, there they were! The whole village came. There were twenty or thirty believers, but there were two to three hundred people there, nonbelievers, watching this celebration of the first church.

Now that's God. This was an area that was unreached. This was an area that no one could get into, even though geographically it was close to where we were, maybe thirty or forty miles. We're not talking of thousands of miles away, but it was an unreached area. Today in that area there are quite a number of churches, where there were none before. God has just opened it up. That happened in the seventies.

About the same time, another young fellow from another church came into my office. He frequently came back and forth and visited with me, because he, like many of these young fellows, sort of looked to me as their teacher.

They called me the guru, and they were the *shisalu*, the disciples of the guru, they were the learners of the teacher. It was a voluntary thing; it wasn't organized in any way. It was just that I was there and they would come and unburden to me, and it's good for a pastor to have someone to unburden to. I frequently wished that I would have had someone that I could have gone to and unburden with the burdens that I had, because sometimes when you're there, you're alone, and you're constantly wishing for someone to share with. So that's what these young pastors were doing. I was their person to whom they could come and share their burdens.

So one day this young fellow from another big church came. He was the senior pastor of a big church. He came and shared with me, and he said, "Sir, I want advice." And that's what he came to me for, frequently. He said, "I feel I have been challenged by a member of my congregation to take the Gospel to the Yanadis." They are another tribal group. "I'm scared," he said.

I said, "You've got a right to be scared. I would be scared, too, if God called me to go to the Yanadis," because they were a totally unreached group again. But they were not like the first group that I just talked about. These were really tribals who lived in trees. They didn't have any dress, and they were shy and violent. They had both temperaments. They were shy, in that they wouldn't talk to people and wouldn't let themselves be seen by people. But they were violent in that, if they did see people, they might kill them. So if you go into that community, you're fortunate if nobody meets you. But if somebody meets you, you may be carried out wounded at the best, or dead.

That was the community, at that time unreached, to which this young pastor said, "God has called me. What's your advice?"

I said, "I can't tell you what to do, I'm not God." I said, "I can't give you clear direction. You know how dangerous it is. My only counsel is, make sure you know it is of God."

Then he shared with me a confirmation of why he believed it was of God, and it did certainly confirm to my mind that it was a calling of God. "Here is the reason I feel called to do this," he said. "There is a man in my congregation who is well educated, has a high position, and he comes from this tribe. He does not know how as a baby he got out of that tribal group. But he got out of that tribal group, was adopted into a family that was not of this tribe, and then became a Christian. But he is of this tribe, and he knows it." In effect, you see, this man in his church was the first Christian from that tribe. He was not saved within the group, but became a Christian outside it.

And the pastor said to me, "It's this man who has come to me and asked me if I would go with him to bring the Gospel back to his own people." That's this Yanadi people.

I said, "All right. My feeling is, then, it would be of God. So I'll come with you."

He said, "No, no, you don't come with us."

I said, "Well, I would like to go, as a senior person."

He said, "No, we'll go," because he knew it was dangerous. Well I knew it was dangerous too. That's why I wanted to go with them, in case I could be of help. As it turned out, it was good that I didn't go, as you'll see.

So the day came when he and this man were ready to go to this tribal group. They got onto a rickshaw. The rickshaw driver brought them to within two miles or so of the village and stopped. He said, "I'm going no further. It's up to you; do whatever you want. I'm going back. You're on your own." So they had to walk. You can't blame the rickshaw driver, because they were headed into a dangerous area.

So they walked in, in fear, but feeling that God wanted them to get into that village to bring the Gospel. They walked in, looked around, and of course this man who was one of them was going to tell them, "I am one of you. And somehow or other as a baby I was brought out, and I'm coming back to bring you Good News."

When they got there, they saw no one, of course, but they knew hundreds of eyes were watching them from the trees. Suddenly an old woman came out—an old, old woman. She screamed, "These are the men!"

Well, naturally they wondered what she meant. Did she mean these are the men we've got to kill, or what?

"These are the men!" She yelled it so that all the people around watching could hear what she said. And then she told them they could follow her. She spoke in the tribal dialect, but it was close enough to Telugu that they could understand. She told them, "I had a dream where two men would come to this village and tell us about the true God. The two men I saw in the dream are you two."

So you see, if I had gone, that dream would not have been fulfilled. There would have been a third person there that should not have been there. So that was of God, and that opened up that village, because now she shared that dream with the village, and now she told the villagers, "Here are the men." And then of course the two of them told the Gospel.

I've talked with them since, and now they tell story after story after story of miraculous works by God within that community: healings, deliverances, miracles, bringing rain when there shouldn't have been rain so that there could be baptisms. I could go on and on with story after story, because I've worked with that evangelist.

He comes into my office every time I'm in India and shares with me what God is doing. The last time he was there, the 87th church in that community was dedicated from that time to now. By the year 2000 God gave him a vision—when did this happen? Was it ten years ago? I'm not clear on my dates on this—but anyway, within a decade...

Joyce: I thought it was around the early '90s.

Bill: Okay. Within a decade or less. He originally shared with me, "God's given me a vision of 100 churches." And it's going to happen within the decade, because they're now at their 87th church. That's God opening up India in the area of evangelism.

Joyce: Also, you should tell what happened when it came to baptizing, and when it came to introducing the Lord's Supper.

Bill: Okay. As I said, I could keep telling incident after incident. At first the village was open because of the dream that this elderly lady had, and so the evangelists got in and the villagers listened. A number came to Christ. They were totally illiterate, but they were taught the Word of God.

And the time came when the new believers were ready for baptism as a public witness to their community. So they asked this pastor, who was now full-time working as an evangelist among them, "We want to be baptized this Sunday." It was the dry season, hot season.

He said, "Well, the nearest river is about four miles away. And," he said, "we'll even have to dig to get water, because the river's almost dry." That happens in dry season. "But," he said, "we may be able to dig a pit where enough water would flow in so that we could baptize you."

They said, "No, no, we're not going to be baptized four miles away. We want to be baptized here in our community. It's a witness to them, not away from them."

The pastor asked, "How can we do it? Where's the water?"

They said, "God will give the water." I mean, they're simple people, so they have a simple trust.

The pastor said to himself, "I don't know what's going to happen," and he went home. This was Thursday or Friday, and the custom among them is that the day that they receive baptism, or the first Sunday after they receive baptism, they get communion. The two things go together. He knew he would have to prepare communion for that Sunday if there was going to be a baptism. But he didn't know whether there was going to be a baptism.

He went home and prayed, "God, what am I going to do? These people want baptism; they want it in their community. It's dry season! If it were rainy season, we could baptize them there, because there are puddles and wells and things all over the place. But they're all dry!" And he went to bed Saturday night, not knowing what to do.

That Saturday night there was an unseasonable downpour of rain in the village, just for an hour or so, a thunderstorm. Sunday he went to the village. They had given a piece of ground to build a church. They had dug part of the foundations, a hole 3 feet by 3 feet by 3 feet. Three feet deep. They had dug that, and when he went there, it was filled with water. That was the baptismal tank, They were baptized right in the partly dug foundation. Now, that's one of the stories in this. But another story in that was…

Joyce: Are you telling about how some old lady or some man had seen what baptism was before they had done it?

Bill: I'm coming to it.

Joyce: There was somebody who understood before that what was going to happen. And what happened with communion.

Bill: There are all kinds of stories; I mean, there are all kinds of instances of God's response to people's faith and prayers, miraculous incidents, one after another. But anyway, the baptism took place in this miraculous way. In other words, these people knew that they had to be baptized in their community, as a witness, not outside their community. That was divine, sovereign revelation knowledge. They weren't reading the Bible, but they had this.

Then, when they were baptized, another elderly lady came to the pastor. She got up and gave a testimony, really, because that's what they do in India. They're spontaneous testimonies; you can't stop them. They'll go on for hours. I mean, they just keep getting up and up, telling what God is doing.

So this woman got up, and said, "I know what is going to happen now." And this pastor looked at her, and said, "What do you mean, you know what is going to happen?" She said, "After this baptism, we're going to have a church service. And the pastor is going to give us bread, and each of us will take bread, and he's going to give us…

Joyce: Red water.

Bill: Red water. And the pastor looked at her, and he said, "Who told you this?"

She said, "I saw it in a dream. And that's what you're going to do now, isn't it?"

He said, "Yes, it is. Do you know what you have described?" That's because now he was going to give the teaching on communion. He hadn't given it; because they hadn't been baptized. That's the way that we go. You teach them, and then when they want baptism, then you teach them communion. He hadn't taught them that. But this woman got it from God, before he gave it, and he said, "That's right, and I've got the bread, and I've got the wine here, and it does speak," and she had got it.

I want to tell an incident of another elderly woman, a woman who had two boys. She became a Christian, and they get a new name in India, when they become a Christian. So this pastor said, "What name do you want?"

She said, "I want the name Sarah."

He said, "Okay, that's a nice name." So she got the name Sarah. A month or two later, her husband got saved. He became a Christian. So when his naming ceremony came, the pastor said, "What name does your husband want?"

She said, "Abraham."

He said, "Fine. Abraham's a good name. Okay, Abraham."

And then later, the two sons got saved. "What name do you want?"

"Isaac and Jacob," they said.

And this pastor looked at her, and he said, "Have you heard this story? Who told you this story?"

She said, "What do you mean? What story?"

He said, "You know, in the Bible, there's an Abraham."

"There is?" she said.

"You know there's a Sarah in the Bible?" he asked.

"Really?" she said.

"You know there's an Isaac? You know there's a Jacob?"

"No," she said.

They had received the names in dreams.

You know, I think that God in a beautiful way was sort of teaching these people who were just then becoming literate through our literacy program; but He was teaching these people, and assuring them that He was the true God.

I could go into other stories. The first death of a Christian in that community is a testimony that's tremendous! Do you want me to tell it?

DB: I can hardly wait!

Bill: It's a tremendous testimony. The church had been growing, and it was some years later. There had been no deaths, and there had been miraculous healings of sickness. But then a young man died, a Christian in the community.

The old traditions in that community, when a person dies, it just becomes total chaos. There's a frenzy of laceration of bodies in order to appease the evil spirits; there are all kinds of noises and stomping and screaming and yelling in order to drive out the demonic forces. And so that is what everybody expected. That's what happens at a death in that community. I can't describe it, but it's demonically chaotic. That maybe is the best description to give of it.

Now here's a Christian who has died. What happens? Everybody in the community was looking. Here's a young man, he's leaving children and he's leaving a wife. The wife is crying, the children are crying, but she's not screaming. She has sorrow from the loss, but she's not yelling. She's not lacerating her body.

And then the relatives who are non-Christians came and said to this young Christian woman, and her children, "Here's what you have to do in order to placate the spirits."

And she said, "No, no, no, we don't do that. He gets buried in a Christian way." And they say, "What's a Christian way?" And so, everybody in that village came to the first Christian funeral. And they looked.

The pastor, of course, preached the Word, telling what happens when a person dies in Christ; but this could have been a tragedy because up until that time God was miraculously healing everybody, and now here was a young evangelist who died. It could have been tragic. You know, the others could have said, "Your God's not powerful." That's what they're looking at in India: Is your God powerful?

So this death could have been a tragedy, but it wasn't. The

widow told her relatives with tears in her eyes, "My husband, I am going to see him again. He has gone to a land that is better, he is now at peace, he has now got joy."

They looked, and they asked, "What is this? How can a woman be so peaceful? She's sorrowful, but how can she be so peaceful? Why are the children not screaming? What is this?"

That first Christian burial was witnessed by that whole community, and the news spread throughout other villages, and through his death there were, I don't know the number, but there were a number of communities that were open to the Gospel for the first time, because they said that this man has a God who must be really, truly powerful.

So God took something that Satan probably thought was going to be chaotic, and God turned it to open up more areas to the Gospel. It was a beautiful thing. The pastor came with tears in his eyes and shared with me. He said, "The first Christian burial was a triumph. We went to the burial place singing songs of triumph! 'Our God Reigns.'" And he said, "When we sang that," he said, "the people were wondering and saying, 'This is a powerful God, because even in death He is strong.'"

DB: That's beautiful.

Bill: Isn't it beautiful? I get so many stories in this that I think, Lord, I could be spending eternity sitting here telling these stories to the glory of the Lord.

Joyce: Let me just say that to understand this better you should know a little about the god that the Yanadis worship. I warn you that it is pretty gross, and Bill did not mention this, but this particular tribal group worship a blood-vomiting god. In their ceremonies, when they get into the frenzy of this, they themselves begin to vomit blood. When they're finished with all that, they go back to being their normal shy, violent selves. That is the group, the Yanadis. And there are a couple million of them in that particular tribal ethnic group. So coming from that to the Lord Jesus Christ, who shed His blood for them, is quite a change.

Bill: Yes, and I think, too, just to continue about God

opening up India, I believe that it was opened up in many ways. I know that there was prayer there, and I know that the Word of God was there, and also through signs and wonders, God moving in real ways, areas were opened up. Really, one does not exclude the other. There's prayer, the Word of God, the teaching, and the signs and the wonders and the miracles. They all go together. It wasn't one without the other.

It is not only by doing miraculous healings, and deliverances, by various kinds of miraculous events, but also this is based upon the Word that has been distributed in India. Through that Word the nation of India and the homes of India have been opened up to the mighty God who is there. So the Word is the basis on which the belief is coming of what God is doing.

There has been the preaching of the Word, and then there have been the lives and testimonies and witnesses of those who are God's servants in India, serving Him. So there is the demonstration of a God who is a life-changing God.

For example, those who were in the caste of thieves, they were born into a caste that stole. Their life was dependent upon stealing, and that's how they lived. God came in and reached that community, saved them, and immediately they stopped stealing and started to work.

Now who taught them to do that? It was the Holy Spirit, and then they saw that was the teaching of the Word of God, "Thou shalt not steal." But even before that, it was the Holy Spirit. So there is also that element of God's working in the community and in the lives of the new believers, changing them, transforming them according to the Word. The community is seeing this, and seeing these wonderful changes.

So there are all of these things working. It is not only the miraculous element, but there is also that element of the depth of the Word, the foundation of the Word, and then the faith in the Word that God has given as it's created by the Holy Spirit, and the lives that are changed through the working of the Holy Spirit.

**DB:** That's beautiful.

**Bill Teate:** And prayer?

**Bill:** Prayer plays a very important part in all that is being done, in all that is happening. As you've asked that now, there is a very vivid demonstration of the power of prayer in opening a community that I heard about, resulting in the birth of a new church. This happened among a caste Hindu community that lived on the other side of the river from the Yanadis.

There was a very strong anti-Christian feeling in this Hindu caste group. They would not allow the Christians into the village. This village was across the river from the Yanadi tribal group. By Hindu custom, the Yanadis literally were not allowed to touch the caste group, nor did the caste group interact with the Yanadis. But this caste group knew that something was happening in this community on the other side of the river. They knew about this outcast people, but they didn't know anything really about the Gospel. They didn't even know the name of the God that they worshipped, but they just knew they had turned from their idols and were worshipping some God.

Now what I am about to tell you came directly to me from the evangelist with whom it happened. I did not see the incident, but the evangelist through whom it happened told me. He said to me, "In that Hindu village we have now planted our 34th church in three years. The others, the first 33, were out among the Yanadis. This was the 34th." And he said, "Do you know how it happened?"

And I said, "No," and he was sharing as he does with me.

He said, "In that village, in one of the younger families, the wife was seriously ill. She had taken all kinds of medication, not only the regular western medication, but also the village medication. She had done both with no result of any kind of healing. She was still on the pathway to death. She had prayed to the priest, they had given their gifts to the temple, they had done all that was required within their caste religion. They had tried everything, including the mantras we talked about earlier. They even tried witchcraft. They had tried all of this, but the lady was still sick. And it was serious; she was sick and not getting better.

She asked her husband, her young husband in this caste group, "Why don't you pray to the God of those people over there across the river, and see what happens?"

He said, "What do you mean? Those are tribal outcast people; we're caste people; our gods are the ones that can do it."

She said, "No, they can't. We haven't asked that God. Ask him."

And the young man went outside, looked up into the sky. He didn't know the name of the God. He said, "Oh, God, that God, God of those people across the river. Heal and touch my wife, if you're the true God."

While he was outside, his wife came out. She had been touched instantly by God. She got out of bed, came out, and said, "I'm healed! Who did you talk to?"

He said, "It's that God, whoever that God is!"

So they called the people from across the river. They said, "Come and tell us: what is the name of your God?" They said, "His name is Jesus." Then the people from the Hindu village said, "That's the God we want to know." And that opened up that anti-Christian caste Hindu village to the Gospel, and within a month there was a new church, a group of believers. Now they've got a mud-and-straw building where they meet.

That's God's power being released in a way that is not traditional. These people were sincere, and he sincerely asked, "that God, whoever you are." And God honored that prayer and said, "Okay."

That's what I'm trying to say. When we start now talking about India opening up and the church of Jesus Christ being built through a demonstration of the power of God in incident after incident after incident. That's what's happening. God is just doing this, in a beautiful way. This is recent, what I just shared now. It was in 1995.

When I say God is moving like this, he's not moving in a vacuum. I'm not trying to say, "This is happening, and all you have to do is sit back and twiddle your thumbs until it occurs."

DB: No. It's not whimsical, but it is by grace.

Bill: It is. And I want to let people know that it's not by man's ingenuity that things are happening, but just by God empowering, and then man being willing to move in that power of God, and things are taking place.

DB: He's responding to the faith of the people, and even to the tentative reaching out of inquiring people, before they have really faith.

Bill: That's right. I could share many experiences, but let me go back to one, when we were in Ongole. When was that?

Joyce: 1975.

Bill: Well, I'm going back now to show the same thing happening in another way. At that time we were in this place called Ongole, working in a hospital. Joyce was in charge of the lab and outreach programs in the hospital, and I was the administrator. In that responsibility I had a very interesting experience where one day a lady came in from a village that was within our area. She came into the office and asked me if I would come and speak at her church in that village.

I was sort of surprised that there was a church in that village, because we, as Baptists, hadn't done any work in that village, and there was a division of regions for mission work. I thought, "Well, how come there's a church there?" She said, "You come and see. We want you to share the Word, any day, any time, we'll make the meeting." So, I didn't have an excuse. She wasn't asking me for a specific date or a specific time, she just said, "Any time you come, we'll have a church meeting."

I set a date, and she said, "You can join us for lunch; we'll have fellowship and lunch afterwards." Well, that was good; I was going to get a good curry and rice out in the village.

When the day came, I got there about ten in the morning. The room was maybe 25 by 30 feet, a fairly good size. People sat on the dirt floor. I didn't count them, but there were maybe thirty or so.

They sat and they sang and they clapped. It was a very

free spirit; much freer than what I was used to at that point in time, as a Baptist minister. It wasn't formal enough for my taste. They were clapping, and I never clapped too much, but I did a bit of it there and found out it wasn't too bad. You could start to enjoy it a bit. And that was the service.

They sang; they knew the hymns. They sang for half an hour, forty-five minutes, as they often do at these services. No one had a watch except me, so nobody really knew what time it was. It was all very informal. I wasn't really sure who was the leader. There didn't seem to be any one person. Just any one would lead out in singing, and they all would sing and clap, and all very joyfully to the Lord.

After about forty-five minutes of singing like this, they started spontaneously to give testimonies. Here again there was no one that stood up and said, "Now we'll have testimonies." A lady just got up and gave a testimony of what God had done. Another lady got up, another man got up, and there was just a period of spontaneous testimonies where you could hardly stop them.

I was impressed with these testimonies. They were in Telugu, and I was there to speak at the meeting in Telugu, so I was following along. I was impressed with all these testimonies because they were talking about what God had done in the now. Hardly any of them went farther back than 24 hours. It was not yesterday or last month. It was, "This morning God..." It was all what God was doing in the now. And that impressed me. I thought, "These people, they're walking with God in the now." If I gave a testimony, I'd go back to the 20th of February 1942. God saved me. I would be going way back and telling things. They just were telling of what God was doing in their lives.

Then one lady got up during that testimony period and said, "This morning when I was preparing breakfast [that would be about 5 to 6 o'clock in the morning, the normal time], God spoke to me and told me to go down and pray for the Hindu man who is sick." They all knew who she was talking about. She said, "God spoke to me and said, 'Go and pray for him, now.'" So she said, "I left preparing my breakfast, and I went down to the house. The lady, his wife was there, and I told the wife, 'God has told me to come and pray for your husband who's sick.' She said, 'Come and pray for him.'"

Then this lady said, "I prayed for him. When I prayed for him, God instantly healed him." Of course, they all were praising God, and she said, "Then I led him and his wife to Christ. They became new creatures in Christ." She sat down. That was her testimony. I thought, "Oh, God, that's really something that this happened!"

As soon as she sat down, a man got up. He said, "That's right, I'm that man." He said, "This morning, six o'clock, I was a sick Hindu. Now I'm a healthy Christian. God touched my life!"

I saw in that little group of believers an unleashed power of God, a power of witnessing. They were all talking about how God used them to be witnesses. I've pulled out the most dramatic one to share with you. But they were all about God moving in everyday living. And as I said, those testimonies did not go back farther than 24 hours, talking about how God had done something in each of the lives of those that were testifying.

The end of all of this, of course, was that I had to give my message. Somebody said—it was after about two hours—"Oh, the missionary's here!" I was sitting in the comer. They said, "The missionary's here. We asked him to come and give the message." And I thought, "Yes, and to have lunch, and my lunch time is here!"

They said, "You'd better speak," and I had a good message prepared, but I didn't give it, because God touched my life in that meeting, and I got up and I gave a testimony, which was almost—it was really a confession. I said, "I need to be ministered to by you this morning, rather than my ministering to you." I gave a testimony. I said, "I had a message prepared, but it's not appropriate, because the power that I have heard about in God through you, that's the power that I need in my life. I would ask you to pray for me, because I need that." And so mine was a sharing rather than a message, not of a testimony of what God did in the last 24 hours, but of a need in my own life for what they had.

That's not the end of the story. It would be a good one even if that were the end. But a couple of years later this same lady came to my office. I knew her at once. We talked, and she said, "We'd like you to come and speak at our convention." I said, "At your what?" She said, "Our convention." I said, "A convention means a number of churches." She said, "Yes, that's right." I said, "You had only one church when I was there before, one church in that hall." She said, "That's right. But last year we had a convention, and it was over a hundred churches." I said, "Over a hundred? How many this year?" She said, "We don't know until they come, but maybe 200, maybe three. We want you to come." And I went.

You see, there's an explosion of believers empowered by God, who is demonstrating His power in their everyday living as they pray for the sick and help those who need deliverance. Also in feeding the poor, which some of them did. They were just open to what God was leading them to do. I saw it in that first service, where they said, "God, we are willing to move with You." They moved with God; not only was there a church in that community through that witness, but that community then reached out until there were literally hundreds of churches in the whole of that area, each one witnessing in the power of the Holy Spirit. Now that, as I said, was a long time ago, back in 1975.

DB: You said you were surprised when you heard about the first church. How did that church get planted?

Bill: Basically through the witness of this lady and her husband. They were believers who were moving in the power of the Spirit. But they didn't think there was anything unusual about it. That was just normal Christianity, as far as they were concerned.

DB: And the expansion to several hundred churches? That also happened without foreign missionaries?

Bill: Yes, and without foreign money. Somebody planted the seed, several may have watered; but God gave the increase. So these stories to me are very positive demonstrations of the power of prayer.

There was a man who prayed to Jesus, not knowing he was praying to Jesus, and the power of God was released through that prayer. And that to me is a very, very vivid example, living example, and a church being born out of that, a living example of the power of prayer.

So I believe that what God is teaching in India is temperance. It's not all signs and wonders and the moving of the Spirit, but it is that coupled with the Word, and coupled with the power of God in positive Christian ethical living.

All of these together are very positive, because the Word without the Spirit will make you dry up. The Spirit without the Word will make you blow up. The Spirit and the Word combined helps you grow up. That is in the Lord. That's one of my little sayings.

DB: I like it! I like it a lot! I will use that!

Bill: I'm finished!

*******

But he's not, of course! Nor is Joyce. Far from it; they are hard at work, spiritually, mentally, and physically, carrying out ministries to which God has called them, and listening for fresh calls. I'll never forget the day that our talk about India led them into a burden for getting those Bible cross-stitch pieces onto the walls of American motel rooms, just because we were working in a motel room. The Scotts never stop, and their vision never stops. You have probably noticed as this story has unfolded that neither one of them has ever been content to follow the usual pattern of doing one job and going home after work. I'm not sure they could.

Spreading God's Word in India is the core ministry, but if it prompts them to try to get God's Word into American motels and resort hotels, they'll add that to their long list of projects, always stimulating the enthusiasm of others, and enlisting others, so that they can continue using the astonishing gifts God has given them to keep His work growing and spreading.

To partner with them can cost you as little as a contribution, and every contribution you make will bless you as well as the ministry. But if you let it cost you a little more, it will bless you a little more.

Are you part of a group that would like to transform a village in India by banding together to bring good news to the poor through Bible-based literacy? Could you introduce your pastor and your church to the "rice bags" or to the miraculous multiplication plan? What will your part in this work of God be?